Will You Dance With Me?

Experiencing Grace on the Dance Floor

By
Barbara Quillen Egbert

Copyright © 2025 by Barbara Quillen Egbert

All rights reserved.

No part of this book may be reproduced, distributed, or transmitted in any form or by any means, including photocopying, recording, or other electronic or mechanical methods, without the prior written permission of the author, except in the case of brief quotations embodied in critical reviews and certain other noncommercial uses permitted by copyright law.

ISBN: 978-1-969021-13-8 (eBook)

ISBN: 978-1-969021-11-4 (Paperback)

ISBN: 978-1-969021-12-1 (Hardcover)

DEDICATION

I would like to acknowledge and honor the studio professionals who assisted me on my ballroom dance journey: Charisma, Christopher, Chante', Serge, Kyle, Michelle, Sean, John, Matt, Amanda, Mandy, Christina, Jessica, Kristen, Curt, Drew, Gonzolo, Bella and Nicolae.

Sketches on pages 1 and 240 are by Wilson Ong.

Photos included are from Maude Productions, from public platforms of fellow dancers Tran Ho, Mike Humphries, Crystal Domenech, Susan Johnson, and BN Dance Studio, and from my personal collection.

Sadly, none of the photos capture the dazzling brilliance and shimmer of the fabric and crystal embellishment of ballroom dresses.

Scriptures included are from The Holy Bible and taken from various versions.

Table of Contents

INTRODUCTION 1
OVERVIEW 5
THE NEWCOMER 7
   I just have to dance! 9
   The man invites the woman to dance. 11
   The man is the frame; the woman is the picture. 13
   The man's purpose is to make the woman look beautiful 15
   The man's role is to lead; the woman's role is to follow. 17
   The woman trusts the man to lead. 19
   You can dance more fully with two than with one. 21
   Connection is key to a dance partnership. 23
   The goal of the dance couple is to move as a unit. 25
   There are no mistakes in dance. 27
   Grace smiles. 29
   After basic steps are learned, dancing from the heart follows. 31
   Hold your own frame up. 33
   Progression from dependence to independence 35
   Each individual dances with equal ownership. 37
   Equal and Mutual. 39
   The woman mirrors the man. 41
   Exposure to a variety of dance styles 43
   A dance community is formed. 45
   Every person is unique and special. 47
   I love watching you dance. 49
   Welcome back! 51
BRONZE LEVEL 53
   Strength and Beauty 55
   Establish a solid foundation. 57
   The frame provides safety and freedom. 59
   You are a dancer. 61
   Instructors personalize a student's learning plan. 63
   Get out of your head. 65
   Dance is simple, but it's not easy 67

You are dancing beautifully right where you are................................69
Trust the instructors and follow their example. 71
I believe in you more than you do. 73
I see your potential...75
Don't compare your dance journey with another person........77
I choose to stretch and grow. 79
Correction and critique benefit my growth.............................81
I'm proud of you...83
Listen to me. 85
Practice what is learned. 87
Be beautiful...89
You haven't learned it until you can do it yourself. 91
I'm not afraid anymore. 93
The man wears the number on his back..................................95
Keep your eyes on me..97

SILVER LEVEL 99
Layers are built upon a solid foundation. 101
Increased connection 103
That's the best you've ever done. 105
I see you as my partner. 107
Use your partner's strength... 109
You dance too safe... 111
The man's role is to make the woman feel safe................... 113
Sacrifice is required. 115
I've got you. I won't allow you to fall.................................. 117
Keep moving in the direction the Lead initiates. 119
I'm getting better every day! 121
Growing in strength 123
Go out and shine.. 125
I need more from you. 127
A collision of journeys.. 129
I could never be mad at you.. 131
I won't let you give up on yourself....................................... 133
I've been there. 135

Do not be discouraged. ... 137
I'm sorry. Please forgive me. ... 139
A safe place to fail ... 141
You just need more floor time. ... 143
I love you. ... 145
GOLD LEVEL ... 147
Hearts beat as one. ... 149
How are you doing today? ... 151
Be you! ... 153
There is freedom in the lead. ... 155
Experienced dancers know how to wait. ... 157
Dance is a lifelong journey. ... 159
Release ... 161
The student reflects the quality of instruction received. ... 163
She's my student. ... 165
Don't anticipate the lead. ... 167
The Follower keeps inviting the Lead. ... 169
Permission granted ... 171
I just want to dance! ... 173
I'm so happy for you! ... 175
I'm reminding you that you said 'yes'. ... 177
People are rewarded for what they practice in private. ... 179
You are capable of more than you think. ... 181
I want to brighten your day. ... 183
I feel the most free when I am dancing ... 185
Celebrate! ... 187
You took my breath away. ... 189
I want to listen to one voice. ... 191
Onwards and Upwards ... 193
FREE DANCING ... 195
Newcomer, Bronze, Silver, and Gold ... 197
Commencement ... 199
My Debut ... 201
Let's try it! ... 203

If you think I can do it, I trust you!	205
I refuse to derail.	207
Redeem the time.	209
Please come back to dance.	211
Please try better.	213
This is the new rule now.	215
Fill up the space.	217
Hold your core.	219
Different expressions of music	221
1 + 1 = 1 (in dance)	223
Pass by me; surpass me.	225
You're ready!	227
Everything ugly can become beautiful.	229
Competition mode	231
Muscle memory	233
He's our main man.	235
I'm a ballroom dancer.	237
My collection of dresses	239
She's one of Mine.	241
To my fellow dancers with Jesus	245

INTRODUCTION

Will you dance with Me?

During a period of time when I was evaluating the foundation of my relationship with Jesus, I had a dream that was an undeniable invitation from Jesus. In the vision, He extended His hand and asked *Will you dance with me?* Not only did the encounter change my journey with Jesus (which I saw through new eyes as an invitation to *The Eternal Dance*), but it also became the foundation of my book, *Portrait of a Woman and Jesus,* published in 2011. In the process of writing about the encounters women had with Jesus, I began the journey of discovering the heart of Jesus and His Father, encapsulated by the word *Grace*.

It seems as if I have dabbled in dance for most of my life because, for some reason, dance has always been in my heart. As a child, dance lessons were unavailable, but surprisingly (because I had no previous dance training), I was selected to be on my college dance team (very small audition pool), and my love of and for dance began to grow.

While majoring in Physical Education, I explored cheerleading, dance exercise, tap dance, and ballet and organized a recreational children's dance program. I also participated in social dance for several years at summer camp. As a P.E. major with a Teaching Certification and experience with cheerleading and dance team coaching, I landed a job as Color Guard Director at a very large Texas high school. I offered an *Introduction to Dance* class for P.E. credit, introducing the students to an overview of a variety of dance styles with the intent of planting a lifelong love of dance.

After relocating to California in 2005, I signed up for adult ballet, tap, swing, and Zumba offered by the city recreation department. During this time, I began to watch the TV shows *Dancing With the Stars* and *So You Think You Can Dance*. The ballroom dance seed had been planted.

In 2013, after a particularly draining season of life, I stepped into the Costa Mesa Arthur Murray dance studio, and my ballroom dance journey began. The instructor assigned to me was Serge. After the first few classes, I started writing down *Sergisms*—brief statements Serge casually made that related to dance lessons. Initially, these foundational statements related to my dance experience, but I soon connected these statements as analogies to my spiritual journey of dancing with Jesus and the concept of this book was born.

Because of the inherent and foundational purpose of ballroom dance, I've learned that when applied to the spiritual journey of dancing with Jesus, *The Eternal Dance* is placed in our hearts and is based on *Grace*. When life is seen through the lens of our invitation to participate in *The Eternal Dance*, the physical analogies of the journey on the ballroom dance floor are profound.

Though this book is written to share some of the key concepts of ballroom dance (maybe giving a novice a new awareness of the activity), my greater purpose is for the reader to see how *dancing with Jesus* is based on His heart of Love and how He extends *Grace* to us as we journey through life. Maybe this book will also give a novice to dancing with Jesus awareness of what an invitation to *The Eternal Dance with Jesus* might look like.

As you journey through this collection of personal observations—learning about the wonderful world of ballroom dance and especially how it relates to *dancing with Jesus*—I pray that you will be enlightened by the overarching theme of *Grace* and how living a life of *grace* can profoundly impact those around you.

This book is the record of *my* insights on the dance floor, but it would greatly encourage me to know that you, the reader, have benefited from my observations. Two of my closest friends, Amber and Jennifer, encouraged me to include specific suggestions on how to apply touches of *grace* to those in your sphere. Please feel free to use the margins or free spaces to write *your* insights that have been inspired by reading this journey of *dancing with Jesus* and being transformed by *Grace*.

OVERVIEW

Experiencing Grace on the Dance Floor

The sequential entries in the book reflect the continuity of my dance journey, from my first days as a Newcomer—to my choice to intentionally begin the learning process at the Bronze level—to my continuing growth as I faced the challenges of the Silver level—to my goal of reaching the Gold level of skill and eventually dancing freely and unencumbered from my heart with my unique personality.

Each entry of this book is divided into three sections that include physical, spiritual, and relational insights:

> ***On the Dance Floor*** implies simple elegance or refinement of physical movement: elegance · poise · gracefulness · finesse · suppleness
>
> ***Dancing with Jesus*** relates to how we experience spiritual *Grace*: the free and unmerited favor of God, as manifested in the salvation of sinners and the bestowal of blessings.
>
> ***From Grace to Grace*** is the relational giving of *grace* to others as we have experienced and are transformed by the *Grace* of Jesus.

On the Dance Floor:

The insights shared are specific to my ballroom dance journey as it progressed. Though it is my unique journey, those who have been exposed to ballroom dance will probably relate to the phrases and details of the entries.

Observations are specific to the ballroom dance floor experience, but many of the phrases are common to other arenas of growth, such as in sports and the workplace, or as related to parenting and other relationships.

Ballroom dance is a partner activity. Therefore, my dance journey has been experienced within relationships, specifically with my instructors.

Dancing with Jesus:

Because the book title is the phrase Jesus spoke to me in a dream, I have seen my dance journey through the lens of what it might be like to *dance with Jesus*. With dance, there is an invitation. The basis for this book is the assumption that the invitation to *dance with Jesus* has been accepted and the journey of relationship with Him has begun.

The spiritual *dance with Jesus* speaks to relationships, so the analogies drawn relate to how I experience Jesus as an Instructor, Partner, and Friend during my journey.

From Grace to Grace:

As explained in 2 Timothy 1:9, *He [Jesus] has saved us and called us to a holy life—not because of anything we have done but because of his own purpose and grace. This grace was given to us in Christ Jesus before the beginning of time.*

Out of his fullness, we have all received grace in place of grace already given (John 1:16). Therefore, as I have *experienced grace on the dance floor* and within my relationship with Jesus, my mindset and filter with which I interact with others is the result of an overflow of *grace*.

Because *grace* is an uncommon and atypical human reaction, once a person has truly experienced the *Grace* of Jesus, it is transformational. A *grace*-filled person's primary role in life is to encourage others in their personal journey with Jesus.

Though this book is about *my* personal invitation to dance with Jesus and experience His *Grace*, I encourage you to read this book through the lens of *your* personal invitation to *dance with Jesus* and experience His Love and *Grace*.

THE NEWCOMER

A Newcomer to dance attends several studio sessions to get a taste of the ballroom dance experience. The common reason a person wants to learn to dance is so that he or she will feel more comfortable dancing in social situations. Some individuals are looking for a community of new friends and anticipate that through dance activities, they will meet people with a shared interest in dance while learning in a comfortable environment. Some couples are preparing for their wedding dance.

A beginning ballroom dance student is introduced to the fundamentals within a social dance or group setting. Foundational etiquette and roles of the man and woman are practiced while basic patterns are learned. The Newcomer initially begins in a *closed* frame.

A variety of dance styles are introduced so that the new dancer can begin to determine his or her own dance path based on individual interests. Some dancers choose to enjoy the social aspects of the dance community. Others begin to progress through the dance curriculum, emphasizing their favorite dance style. Some dancers choose to focus on *Smooth* styles, such as waltz, foxtrot, Viennese waltz, quickstep, and tango. Others may prioritize *Rhythm* or *Latin* dances of cha-cha, rumba, swing, bolero, samba, paso doble, or jive. *Specialty* dances related to country music, disco, West Coast swing, and salsa are also popular.

Newcomer protocol at my first competition prevented me from wearing an official ballroom dress, so I chose one of my favorite dresses that was blue and had a fancy hem that would swing with the dance movement.

I just have to dance!

On the Dance Floor:

The impetus for me to begin ballroom dance lessons was a product of several converging themes. When Jesus asked, *Will you dance with Me?* the desire to dance was affirmed and began to flourish. Several television dance competition shows became my favorites and solidified my interest in ballroom dance. I had enjoyed dance from the perspective of a spectator, but something compelled me to become a participant.

Even in my older years, I was drawn to dance because I knew deeply in my heart that I was created to dance. Stepping into the studio for the first time, though exciting, was also terrifying. When asked why I was there, I replied with tears, *I just have to dance!*

I was up for the challenge, but I had no idea how transformational the journey would be. Fears would be faced and conquered. I would have to defend my heart's desire to dance to those who did not understand, and I would be stretched physically, emotionally, and mentally. Most importantly, I would be introduced to spiritual parallels of dance in such a significant way that the idea for this book was born.

And so my journey began. *I just have to dance!*

Dancing with Jesus:

Because God has *set eternity in the human heart* (Ecclesiastes 3:11), I believe each of us experiences a tug, whether consciously or unconsciously, to *dance with Jesus* for eternity. Though I have pursued the physical activity of dance, which draws me spiritually closer to God, each of us has unique personalities that are enriched through a variety of activities. Some are drawn into a deeper relationship with Jesus through nature, through creative outlets, or through serving by using their gifts.

No matter what avenue speaks to us spiritually, as we encounter Jesus, we understand more of His Love and *Grace*. During each session in the studio, I would experience *dancing with Jesus* in tangible and parallel ways that transformed my spiritual life.

When presented with the opportunity to play a significant role in eternity, Jesus' mother, Mary said, *Let it be as you said* (Luke 1:38). The path was unknown, but she trusted in faith. And though I had no idea my spiritual relationship would be so profoundly enhanced through dance, I just knew *I had to dance with Jesus*. I embraced the unknown, trusting Him with the process.

Let's begin! *It is time to dance* (Ecclesiastes 3:4).

From Grace to Grace:

Experiencing *Grace* has a profound impact on a person, whether on a human level, such as on the dance floor, or on a spiritual level in a relationship with Jesus. Experiencing *Grace* is transforming. I'm learning to see others through the eyes of God's *Grace* and attempt to live a lifestyle of *grace*, sharing lessons and insights learned with others while encouraging them in their journeys with Jesus.

The man invites the woman to dance.

On the Dance Floor:

The first lesson learned as a Newcomer involves the relationship between the man and woman as they step into partnership. The man extends his left hand to the woman as an invitation to dance.

The first instruction I heard given to men in a group class was, *Be a gentleman. Present your hand and let her step into the frame as closely as she wants. Don't force yourself on the woman. Don't pull her into you. Don't muscle her around the dance floor. Be a gentleman.*

As a woman, it was comforting to hear those words. The man was not to impose his role as Leader on the woman or use his strength to pull her to a level of intimacy she didn't feel comfortable with. The man waits for the woman to respond. It is the woman's choice to accept the invitation and to determine the level of closeness and body contact.

Dancing with Jesus:

Because we were created for relationships and can dance more fully with two than with one, Jesus has invited us into a relationship with Him. He extends His hand and invites, *Come and follow Me* (Matthew 4:19). The invitation to journey with Jesus has been presented to all, but free will plays a role in our relationship. It is our personal choice to accept His invitation and step into the level of intimacy one is comfortable with.

Jesus is a gentleman and will not impose Himself upon a person. He asks, *Will you dance with Me?* Then, He creates a safe place for a person to begin the journey.

Maybe you have been burned by religion and hesitate to accept the invitation to the relationship. Jesus *graciously* waits and moves to the level of intimacy each person feels safe with, giving *Grace and space* for the person to develop trust over time.

From Grace to Grace:

When you live from a foundation of *grace* within a relationship, there is freedom of intimacy. Individuals are joined by choice, not imposed upon.

Individuals should be free to be in relationships at a level that is genuine and comfortable—not enmeshed, needy, or clingy. *Grace* gives and creates safe parameters for a relationship within which both persons can thrive.

The invitation to be within the relationship of another should be in the context of *Grace* received by Jesus. Within *grace,* there is no room or place for domination or control because *grace* offers freedom.

The man is the frame; the woman is the picture.

On the Dance Floor:

The man invites the woman to dance by presenting a frame of his outstretched arms. This stance provides the foundational strength of the partnership. As she steps into the frame, his arms close around her. It is the man's role to consistently hold his frame so that the woman can dance beautifully within the context of a reliable frame.

The man's role is to present the woman as the focus of the partnership. He is the framework for presenting the woman as a beautiful picture.

Dancing with Jesus:

Jesus is referred to as the *chief, chosen, and precious cornerstone* (Ephesians 2:20, 1 Peter 2:6). Our foundation is built on Him because *no one can lay any foundation other than the one already laid, which is Jesus Christ* (1 Corinthians 3:11).

Essentially, Jesus is our reliable and consistent frame. He has invited us into a relationship with Him for the sole purpose of transforming us into a beautiful picture that reflects Him.

But we all, with unveiled faces, beholding as in a mirror the glory of the Lord, are being transformed into the same image from glory to glory, just as by the Spirit of the Lord (2 Corinthians 3:18).

From Grace to Grace:

As we experience the *Grace* of Jesus, our perspective and purpose change because of His foundational strength given to us.

When we reflect the *Grace* of Jesus, *His* purpose of providing foundational strength to individuals so that they can grow and become a beautiful picture becomes *our* purpose. We can testify to the foundation of *Grace* that comes from Jesus and then provide strength and support to others so that they can thrive.

Grace focuses on others with the goal of assisting them in their journey of growth. We do this as parents when we provide a foundational culture of love and *grace* within which children flourish. We do this as friends and partners when we provide others with encouragement and support during their life journey.

The man's purpose is to make the woman look beautiful.

On the Dance Floor:

Because the woman is the picture, the primary goal of the man is to showcase the woman and present her in the most beautiful light. Everything he does is to facilitate her success. To the degree he understands, his role will determine the strength of the partnership. Essentially, the man looks good to the degree he makes the woman look good.

The man uses his foundational strength to make the woman look beautiful. When both individuals in the partnership understand this underlying philosophy, they can dance more fully and freely. The woman learns to rely on her partner's frame and the man learns to focus on making the woman dance successfully—beautifully.

Dancing with Jesus:

The woman is the glory of man (1 Corinthians 11:7). The woman is the reflection of a man's glory. When she looks beautiful, it is a glorious reflection of him.

We are reminded that Jesus, our foundation, has provided the only way to be spiritually successful. One of His purposes is to *present the Church* [and us as individuals] *to Himself in glorious splendor, without spot or wrinkle or anything like that, but holy and blameless* (Ephesians 5:27). Jesus' goal is to make us beautiful so that we reflect His glory.

Now to Him who is able to protect you from stumbling and to make you stand in the presence of His glory, blameless and with great joy, to the only God our Savior, through Jesus Christ our Lord, be glory, majesty, power, and authority before all time, now and forever. Amen (Jude 1:24-25).

And when Jesus' goal of presenting His beautiful Bride, His Church, to His Father, it brings Jesus glory.

From Grace to Grace:

Experiencing the focus of *Grace*—facilitation of our growth and transformation into a beautiful reflection of Jesus—changes how we see ourselves and others. *Grace* becomes our underlying relational style. Our purpose is to facilitate the growth and success of others, unveiling the beauty that God sees.

When you encourage others, cheer them on, and celebrate their victories, you embody *grace*. Though this is not your motivation (because *grace* is from the heart and not contrived), you realize that as you contribute to the beauty (success) of another, it increases your beauty. And *when your light shines, and others see your good works, they give glory to God* (Matthew 9:16).

The man's role is to lead; the woman's role is to follow.

On the Dance Floor:

For a successful partnership, both man and woman understand their primary roles. The man steps into an active role as Leader, accepting the primary responsibility to lead the woman on the dance floor, navigating around the obstacles while communicating the sequence of dance steps.

The woman accepts her role as a Follower, allowing the man to be the primary Leader. As she submits to and trusts his role, this allows her the freedom to dance more fully from her heart because she doesn't have to worry about the safety or strategy of navigating the dance floor. She can thrive within the context of the man leading with his strength—so that she can look beautiful.

Dancing with Jesus:

Just as with our physical dance partner, when we understand the reason that Jesus leads, we can relinquish control, knowing that His leading is in our best interest. When we understand the *Grace* and Love behind Jesus' guidance, we can submit to the process, trusting His role in making us spiritually dance with beauty.

We are reminded that though a person may stumble, *he or she will not fall because the Lord upholds him with His hand* (Psalm 37:24). When we realize that Jesus is our Rock and Fortress, we ask that He *lead and guide us by His good Spirit* (Psalm 31:3). We can trust that He will *lead us on level ground* (Psalm 143:10).

Jesus said that if we want to be His disciple, we must *deny ourselves* (relinquish control) *and follow Him* (Matthew 16:24). *Because He is the Light of the world, whoever follows Him will never walk in darkness but will have the light of life* (John 8:12). *He will lead them to springs of living water* (Revelation 7:17).

From Grace to Grace:

During our lives, we play both Leader and Follower roles. In an ideal world, we are in relationships to promote the growth of each other. As we can trust the genuine motives of a partner, we can surrender to the process and be free to grow.

And as we understand that our greatest role is to provide strength and encouragement to others, we assist in their journeys. This is most evident in the relationship between parent and child. Our goal is to build trust in young lives so that they trust our leadership and guidance.

As you experience the Love and *Grace* extended to you by Jesus, you are better equipped to pass on that love and *grace* to those who are dancing with and beside you in life.

Where are you most aware of the relationship between Leader and Follower? When are you a Leader? When are you a Follower? What are you learning about the role of *grace* within a relationship?

The woman trusts the man to lead.

On the Dance Floor:

In the beginning stages of dance, the woman primarily dances in a *closed* frame, facing in the opposite direction she is traveling—essentially dancing blindly. She trusts the man to guide her around the dance floor. He will lead her in the steps and patterns as well as lead her in the direction of travel—backwards, sideways, or forwards.

The woman learns to relinquish control to the man, the Leader. It might be easier to trust a professional, the pro, than a fellow student, but either way, the growth process requires learning to follow the lead of every male partner. By trusting her pro or amateur partner and allowing him to lead, she communicates that she honors his role. She becomes a partner in developing his skills of leading while she develops her skills in following. Each person's goal is the same—to dance beautifully as a couple.

Dancing with Jesus:

One would think it would be easy to trust Jesus and relinquish control to Him. After all, He knows all, sees all, has our best interests at heart, and has pure motives toward us. The more we understand Who He is, the more we can trust Him. There are times, though, when we forget our dance roles (as a Follower) and attempt to navigate on our own.

During those times when we take matters into our own hands and attempt to manage life, the following verses remind us to trust Jesus:

The Lord is my strength and my shield; my heart trusts in Him, and He helps me. My heart leaps for joy, and with my song, I praise Him (Psalm 28:7).

Let the morning bring me word of Your unfailing love, for I have put my trust in You. Show me the way I should go, for to You I entrust my life (Psalm 143:8).

Trust Me. Follow Me.

From Grace to Grace:

Throughout our lives, we will be given opportunities to lead and follow. We attempt to do so with *grace*. When we lead, our goal is to assist the growth journey of another. At other times, we intentionally surrender our *leading* to another so that the person grows in leadership skills. Acquiescing is passive. Choosing to relinquish control for another to lead is active and says to the partner, *I believe in you and support you in this aspect of your growth journey.*

You can dance more fully with two than with one.

On the Dance Floor:

One way ballroom dance differentiates itself from other forms of dance is due to the partnership of one male dancer and one female dancer. Because two persons are involved, both can use their partner's strength to do things that a person would not physically be able to do while dancing solo.

In addition to the physical benefits of a partnership, a ballroom dancer can also enjoy a fuller level of dance because a relationship is formed. A partnership requires communication and trust. Conflict can arise, but the bond of friendship that develops is a witness to the transformational journey that occurs.

Dancing with Jesus:

In the beginning, a relational God (*Let Us make humans in Our image* from Genesis 1) created a relationship when the man Adam and the woman Eve were joined together to be one. Adam was previously told that he was incomplete without a woman—a partner and a suitable helper. Through the designed partnership of husband and wife, they were mutually and equally commissioned to be fruitful and rule (Genesis 1:26-28, 2:18).

The wisdom of Solomon reminds us that *two are better than one, because they have a good reward for their labor. For if one of them falls, the other one will lift up his companion* (Ecclesiastes 4:9-10).

Dancing solo, apart from Jesus, is also limiting. We can live more fully and completely when walking with Jesus than when on our own. *If you remain in Me* [Jesus] *and I in you, you will bear much fruit; apart from Me, you can do nothing* (John 15:5).

From Grace to Grace:

There is much to be said for developing friendships and partnerships as we walk through life. We were created to be in a relationship, not only with other humans but primarily with God. When we understand the importance and value of relationships, our lives are enriched in numerous ways. This is not to say that living within relationships is easy because there will be challenges. But as we live with *Grace* (Jesus), we learn to live more *gracefully* and *graciously* within all our relationships.

For those of us introverts, it might seem easier not to risk entering into a friendship or relationship because of potential conflict. Can you courageously seek out friendships, knowing that your life will be enhanced by the connection that is developed over time?

You might see or know of someone who avoids relationships. Can you invite that person into a sphere of connection so their life is more complete?

Connection is key to a dance partnership.

On the Dance Floor:

The connection between the Leader (the man) and the Follower (the woman) is established primarily through frame and hand communication. As the couple progresses in their partnership, body connection also plays an important role. A woman's main assignment and primary responsibility is to keep/maintain the connection by consistently pressing or leaning into hand, frame, and body contact points so that she can receive and respond to clues from the Leader regarding direction and steps.

Because the man's main role is to direct/redirect the woman throughout the dance, it is more difficult for him to do so effectively and efficiently if the connection between them is inconsistent or broken.

Dancing with Jesus:

Through connection to Jesus, we maintain communication. As His followers, it is our main job to stay connected to Jesus so that we can hear His voice. Jesus gives us the analogy of branches that are connected—attached to a vine.

I am the vine; you are the branches. If you stay attached to Me and I in you, you will bear much fruit; apart from Me, you can do nothing. Stay united with Me, as I also stay united with you. No branch can bear fruit by itself; it must stay attached to the vine. Neither can you bear fruit unless you stay attached to Me (John 15:4-5).

Over time we grow in the nuances of connecting with our dance partner, Jesus. If there is a *disconnect* within the partnership, it is typically because we need to reassess the importance of reestablishing a connection with Jesus, tuning into His voice, and listening for His lead. We maintain a consistent connection with Jesus through prayer (two-way communication with Him) and reading His Word.

. . . Your hand will lead me, Your right hand will hold me (Psalm 139:10).

From Grace to Grace:

Communication plays a critical role in the success of any relationship and must be mutually established. *Grace* listens to the voice and heart of another, receiving signals as to motive and intent. Just as with our relationship with Jesus, it takes time to develop and maintain communication. It is not a one-way style of communication. Intimacy is two-way communication, with the hearts and souls of both individuals connected.

Does this focus on communication encourage you to reestablish or deepen your connection with a friend?

The goal of the dance couple is to move as a unit.

On the Dance Floor:

The more quickly the man (Leader) and woman (Follower) understand and accept their respective roles, the more quickly the partnership is established. Some women may have difficulty relinquishing control of the partnership to the man, but the skill of following is not a sign of weakness or incapability. Surrendering the lead to the man empowers the man to step into his primary role. And it will free up the woman to concentrate on dancing more fully and beautifully.

The more quickly the woman learns to stay connected and respond to the man's communication, the more quickly the couple will be able to dance as a unit. As a couple begins to trust each other in their respective roles and remain connected, they begin to move together as one.

Dancing with Jesus:

From the beginning of time, the primary example of unity—of oneness, of dancing together—is of a partnership of man and woman in marriage. Jesus confirmed this when He said, *Haven't you read that at the beginning* the Creator *'made them male and female,' and said, 'For this reason, a man will leave his father and mother and be united to his wife, and the two will become one flesh'? So they are no longer two but one flesh.* (Matthew 19:4-6).

Another example of unity—as oneness—is that of Jesus and His heavenly Father. *I and the Father are one* (John 10:30). In His final prayer before His trial and death, Jesus demonstrated the unity He had with His Father. *My prayer is not for them alone. I pray also for those who will believe in Me through their message, that all of them may be one, Father, just as You are in Me and I am in You. May they also be in Us so that the world may believe that You have sent me. I have given them the glory that You gave Me, that they may be one as We are one—I in them and You in Me—so that they may be brought to complete unity. Then the world will know that You sent me and have loved them even as You have loved Me* (John 17:20-23).

Jesus desires unity and oneness with us, just as He has unity and oneness with His Father. When we enter into a relationship with Jesus, our example of unity and oneness is a compelling witness to the world.

From Grace to Grace:

One of the outcomes of living with *grace* is unity and oneness within a relationship. As you learn the roles of leading and following, connection and communication, you reap the fruit of unity. Not only will you dance more beautifully in your relationships, but the world will be encouraged by an example of a relationship that displays loving unity and oneness.

There are no mistakes in dance.

On the Dance Floor:

During the second or third lesson with my instructor, Serge, I stepped on his foot. *Oops, sorry.* He *graciously* replied, *There are no mistakes in dance.* I clearly had just stepped on his foot, so I had to stop and ask him to explain this puzzling statement. He said that either I didn't know the steps or patterns, or those steps weren't in my muscle memory, or I misread his lead, or I had lost the connection with him.

The statement that *there are no mistakes in dance* was revolutionary for me. What a relief! It gave me the freedom to not be perfect. I wasn't going to disappoint Serge if I didn't do everything correctly (which, in fact, I couldn't).

The journey of dance would be a process of learning steps, implanting them in muscle memory, and learning to read my partner's communication—all with the realization that this would take time. My instructor would be patient with the process, even if it meant that I occasionally stepped on his toes. This lesson on *experiencing grace on the dance floor* probably made the most impact on me and changed my life.

Dancing with Jesus:

When we begin to understand Jesus' heart, it truly is revolutionary and freeing. *God did not send his Son into the world to condemn the world but to save the world through Him* (John 3:17). My eternal dance partner, Jesus, is *for* me, not *against* me. He understands my weaknesses and inadequacies. He still believes in me and is patient with my progress.

Even when I have missteps, He forgives and doesn't abandon me. I think of His example of forgiveness on the cross: *Father, forgive them because they don't know what they are doing* (Luke 23:34).

He has removed our sins from us as far as the east is from the west (Psalm 103:12). He continues to shower me with *Grace*, even when I step on His toes while dancing with Him.

From Grace to Grace:

When you have experienced forgiveness, you understand how *grace* creates a culture of freedom and peace within which to grow. We intentionally attempt to create a culture of *grace* around us and see people through the eyes of Jesus—forgiving their missteps and mistakes and releasing them to go in peace (Luke 7:36-50).

We need to remind ourselves that there are various reasons for missteps caused by others and pray, *Father, forgive them* (when they step on our foot or worse, as in Jesus' case); *they don't know what they are doing.*

Believe the best in people, as Jesus does with us. And be patient with their journey because Jesus is patient with us.

Grace smiles.

On the Dance Floor:

The lesson after the comment *there were no mistakes in dance,* I remember Serge smiling when I stepped on his toes. He knew that my misstep wasn't intentional. With his smile, he graciously granted me the space and time needed to grow and progress. When I saw him smile, I said to myself, *Grace smiles* and reminded myself that I either needed more practice with the pattern because it wasn't in my muscle memory or that I had misread his communication.

Because *Grace smiled*, I began to ask my instructor what I needed to rework or what I had missed. There was freedom in the process because he continued to be patient with me until I could successfully perform the pattern or understand the newly introduced concept.

Dancing with Jesus:

Jesus smiles when we dance with Him, even in our missteps. He knows our frame and story even as we were being formed in our mother's womb (Psalm 139:13-16). Jesus can empathize with our weaknesses and struggles because He was one of us when He walked on the earth and experienced the reality of humanity (Hebrews 4:14-16).

Many of us need to be reminded that *You, Lord, are a compassionate and gracious God, slow to anger, abounding in love and faithfulness* (Psalm 86:15). If we truly believe that Jesus *graciously smiles* upon us while we are dancing with Him, we have the freedom to continue to grow into His image. He forgives and has unending patience with our growth journey as we continue to listen to His instruction.

Though this concept is written within the context of intentionally accepting the invitation to *dance with Jesus*, there are times when we turn our backs on the relationship. *Jesus still smiles*. And just as with the prodigal son, Jesus longingly waits for our return to dance again with Him (Luke 15:11-32). There is no condemnation. *Grace smiles* and waits for our return to the dance.

From Grace to Grace:

Because I have experienced *Grace smiling* at me while I am in the process, I can intentionally give *grace* to others. When you have received God's *Grace* with patience and encouragement on your journey, you learn to smile at others because you realize they are also on growth journeys.

This philosophy of *grace smiles* had a profound impact on me in my role as a parent. A child, no matter the age, is learning, and the process takes time. My goal as a parent is to facilitate growth with the same patience and encouragement I have received on the dance floor and from Jesus. *Grace can smile* within all relationships. You can choose to believe the best in all people, forgive when stepped on, and remain patient as relationships are restored. This may seem naive and unrealistic, but I choose to remind myself that regardless of how I am treated, *Grace smiles* and that I, too, can choose to *smile with grace*.

Where can you apply *grace smiles* in your life?

After basic steps are learned, dancing from the heart follows.

On the Dance Floor:

There are multiple and unending layers to the dance journey. A beginning student first learns the basic steps and patterns while in a closed frame. The beginning student who is a man not only learns the steps and patterns but also how to communicate the *lead* to the woman. The woman learns the basic steps and patterns and also how to respond to and *follow* the man's lead. An interesting and amusing starting point is the woman typically begins a pattern with her right foot because, according to the pros, *the woman is always right*.

Most of the beginning layers of dance involve frame and footwork. As the student progresses, leg, hip, and torso techniques are added. Later in the journey, the techniques progress from head to heart when the dancer translates body actions into emotional expressions of the music.

Dancing with Jesus:

Our relationship with Jesus is a lifelong journey that begins with two basic and seemingly simple steps: *Love God and love others as yourself* (Luke 10:27). But, just as with dance, the beginning Follower of Jesus (whether male or female) soon realizes there are multiple and unending layers to the dance journey.

A new Follower of Jesus begins to walk as Jesus walked, doing what He asks and going where He guides. Over a period of time, *doing* the basics—through trusting obedience—begins to transform how we think and who we become. We learn to dance from the heart. *Grace* transforms our *being*, which translates into dancing fully with Jesus from both head *and* heart.

From Grace to Grace:

When parenting, parameters are put into place for a young child to grow and learn. There are many simple actions that are taught—like saying *please* and *thank you,* looking both ways before crossing a street, and sharing toys. Layers of learning and growth take years of progression. A child doesn't grow up driving a car, but it takes many years of maturity to develop motor skills, social awareness, and trust before a parent turns the keys over to a new driver.

And just as a child learns the *head* aspects of kindness, such as sharing toys, it takes time (and much patient teaching from parents) for the deeper *heart* aspects of kindness to mature.

The parenting and teaching process requires much *grace* and patience. Fundamentals, though seemingly simple, must be learned and practiced (*doing*) before a person can excel and perform from the heart (*being*).

Hold your own frame up.

On the Dance Floor:

Soon after the foundational message to be a Follower sunk in, the next layer of instruction was added. Just because I was a Follower (as the man leads), it didn't mean I was to be a passive participant. On the contrary, the woman (while she follows and maintains connection) provides strength to the partnership by maintaining her own frame.

My instructor helped me to understand that the weight I imposed on his frame by not supporting myself affected his ability to move and was tiring. He was willing to support me in my Newcomer stage, but it was time to move to the next level of dance—that of being responsible for my own frame.

Initially, I enjoyed relying on my partner's frame, as it seemed easier because I could be more passive. Though it took time to develop the strength of my muscles for this new level of dance, I soon felt empowered to know that I was growing in my partnering skills. When both partners hold their own frames up, the movements below the frame have foundational strength, the shape of the *picture* is consistent, and the dance becomes more effortless.

Dancing with Jesus:

The first step in a relationship with Jesus is to surrender control and rely on His *lead*. But my partnership with Jesus is incomplete if I am passive within the relationship. Yes, I *follow*, but there is more. Now, I imitate Him and attempt to do what He does.

Though Jesus' disciples were with Him continually, learning from Him and watching Him in action, there were times when He intentionally sent them out on their own (Matthew 10, Luke 9:1-6). Jesus was stretching them to hold up their own frames. It took time and practice, and they weren't always successful, but their faith grew (Matthew 17:14-20).

We are encouraged to *work out your salvation with fear and trembling, for it is God who works in you to will and to act in order to fulfill his good purpose* (Philippians 2:12-13). We are connected to God, but as an active participant we are continually growing our faith muscles.

From Grace to Grace:

Grace validates the courageous steps others take as they gain strength in their journey. As a parent, you extend *grace* when you encourage your children to *hold their own frame up*. You provide a culture of *grace* that allows your children to grow, even when they occasionally *fall* while in the process of developing their own *muscular strength*. Yes, you are there for them, but you enable growth by saying, *This is your journey. You have what it takes. I'll always be here and support you.*

Progression from dependence to independence

On the Dance Floor:

In the progression of learning, the beginning dancer transitions from being in a *closed* hold to dancing with one hand connected in an *open* hold to occasionally dancing independently side-by-side, though not physically connected or touching.

When in the first level of *closed* hold, the woman is moving backwards, as led by the man. This position felt safe for me because I could rely on the frame and both guiding hands of the man. The next level of *closed* hold was when the pattern required one step forward into the space created by the lead. It took consistent encouragement to own my role and confidently step forward.

The progression from the basic *closed* hold to letting go of one hand was subconsciously frightening. My posture would be more timid and lean forward, as if searching for the safety of the basic hold with my partner. With practice, it became more comfortable to let go of one hand and dance more independently. Eventually, there were steps and patterns that required dancing side-by-side with no hold at all. It required me to own my independence while knowing my partner was still present and beside me.

Dancing with Jesus:

As Jesus grew from a child into a man, there was a progression from dependence to independence. *He became stronger, was filled with wisdom, and the grace of God was on Him* (Luke 2:40). Though His Heavenly Father sent Him out on His saving mission, He was still dependent on His Father.

Just as in dancing, even though *letting go* of one hand, I can trust and depend on my Leader (Jesus) to be there. As Jesus *sends me out*, challenging me to become more independent, we stay connected and continue to dance together. I can trust Him because He knows exactly when to let go and send me out.

Yet I am always with You; You hold me by my right hand. You guide me with your counsel and afterward You will take me into glory (Psalm 73:23-24).

From Grace to Grace:

The natural progression from dependence to independence is a requirement for maturity. The most obvious sphere to watch this process is when a helpless baby, totally dependent, learns to crawl, then walk, feed himself or herself, and eventually is launched into adulthood. You extend *grace* by facilitating the process of growth while standing beside, offering support and encouragement.

One of the greatest gifts you can give to another is to support him or her in their journey from dependence to independence. It is imperative that you discern when and how to let go so that the individual can mature and become the person God uniquely created them to be.

Each individual dances with equal ownership.

On the Dance Floor:

The unity of a ballroom couple is increased when each individual dances with equal ownership. As I grew in my skill level and ability to dance more independently, the partnership became more *equal* and unified. We danced more beautifully and fully as each person took ownership of his or her individual journey.

My strength contributed to the strength and greater potential of our partnership.

Dancing with Jesus:

Jesus calls us to *work just as He works* (John 5:17, 36). My relationship with Jesus is not passive. The more I understand God's will and purpose for me, the more I can join Jesus in His work.

I can do all things through Christ who gives me strength (Philippians 4:13).

Very truly I tell you, whoever believes in me will do the works I have been doing, and they will do even greater things than these, because I am going to the Father (John 14:12).

Jesus does the will of His Father, and as we actively partner with Jesus in His will, we will do even greater things—together as a team.

From Grace to Grace:

All human partnerships are stronger when both individuals participate actively in the relationship. Ideally, a marriage is strengthened when both partners are completely invested in the relationship. Roles might be different, but there is *equal* physical and emotional investment and commitment toward strengthening the team.

The potential for impact of a relational partnership is increased when both individuals are growing independently, yet together as a team. In reality, there may be a time when *grace* needs to be extended to a partner during a time of unequal investment in the relationship. But even during a time of disequilibrium, when you take ownership of *your* aspect of the partnership, strength and growth are still possible.

Equal and mutual

On the Dance Floor:

I have never experienced an activity or community that naturally revolved around and prioritized the equality and mutuality of both sexes. Ballroom dance requires a man and a woman to be equally important and mutually responsible for his or her individual contributions to the partnership.

It seems to me that the ballroom dance environment highlights the perfect blend of men and women—whether students, coaches, judges, and spectators. There might be an increased number of female students because of their interest in dance, but that implies that an equal number of men are also in the studio as instructors.

Because of the equality of roles, I can say that I've never experienced the balance of equality and mutuality of the sexes as in the world of ballroom dance.

Dancing with Jesus:

In the beginning of the human story, the pattern and intent of male and female relationships were recounted in the story of Adam and Eve. Both were created with equal value and mutual and shared responsibility.

Throughout history, this has not been the case, but when Jesus came to earth, He shattered the human norms that went against the created intention. Jesus actually spoke to women (John 4:1-42) and let them touch Him in acts of devotion (Luke 7:37-50; John 12:1-8) and while seeking His healing power (Mark 5:21-24). The Bible related numerous instances when Jesus encountered women with gentleness and respect, elevating their value in the eyes of those watching His interactions. Women were included in Jesus' ministry, and they followed Him as He traveled from town to town, providing financial support (Luke 8:1-3). He appeared first to a woman after His resurrection, commissioning her to tell the other disciples that He had risen.

We all have equal and mutual access to a relationship with Jesus. Yes, we may have different roles—just as in ballroom dance—but the inclusion and valuing of both male and female is undeniable—*for you are all one in Christ Jesus* (Galatians 3:28).

From Grace to Grace:

When you understand the purpose and intent of the equality and mutuality of the sexes, you will work together as partners toward shared goals. Yes, there are differences, but males and females complement each other and can value and respect each person not only for his or her gender but also for his or her unique personality.

When you understand the reality that each person is individually created by God, you value and respect them for the unique being he or she is. You can model what it looks like for a male and female to work together in partnership—whether in the home, the workplace, or the public sphere.

The woman mirrors the man.

On the Dance Floor:

When watching a professional couple (who were also married) dance together, they looked like two individuals dancing as one. During a coaching session, the wife of the pro couple stated, *The woman mirrors the man.*

When facing my male dance partner, it seemed easier to mirror him because I could see his facial expressions, tall posture, and arm styling. Dancing side-by-side was more challenging, but I tried to look in the studio mirror and imitate the style and intensity of my instructor. My goal was to look like him and dance like he did. This was for my personal growth and because I desired to dance as if we were a unit—a team.

When following or *mirroring* the man (the Leader), it was important for me to dance at a slightly slower pace, which gave me a fraction of the time to react to his lead.

Dancing with Jesus:

Jesus is the *radiance, the reflection, of God's glory and the exact representation, or imprint of His being* (Hebrews 1:3).

Because it is my intent to mirror Jesus—as He mirrors His Father—and to be a reflection of His heart and will, I keep my gaze on Him. Instead of rushing ahead, I slow my pace which gives me time to react to His lead and to study the nuances of His expression.

And we all, who with unveiled faces contemplate the Lord's glory, are being transformed into his image with ever-increasing glory, which comes from the Lord, who is the Spirit (2 Corinthians 3:18).

During the process of dancing with Jesus, we put on a new nature that is increasingly *renewed in knowledge of the image of the Creator* (Colossians 3:10).

From Grace to Grace:

When people interact with me, I want them to see the *image or likeness* of Jesus. He is continually transforming me to reflect His heart for His Father and for every person I interact with.

My lifelong focus and goal are to be personally transformed into the glory that comes from Jesus' reflection. And my greatest mission in life is to encourage others in their transformational *dance with Jesus*.

What qualities do you want people to see when you interact with them? Do they witness a reflection of the *Grace* of Jesus? How can you encourage others in *their* transformational *dance with Jesus*?

Exposure to a variety of dance styles

On the Dance Floor:

Music and dance are universal languages because dancing to music expresses the emotions of the heart. Various dance styles have been developed through the years by historical and musical influences, reflecting different nationalities and cultures.

In the ballroom, Waltz, Foxtrot, Tango, Quickstep and Viennese Waltz are considered *Smooth* dance styles. *Rhythm* and *Latin* styles include Cha-cha, Swing, Rumba, Bolero, Mambo, Samba, Paso Doble, and Jive. Additional styles include Salsa, Bachata, West Coast Swing, Disco, and Country Western (as shown in the photo of fellow dancer Cindy).

The well-rounded dancer will have been exposed to a variety of dance styles and will develop an appreciation for different cultures.

Dancing with Jesus:

Jesus was sent to be *Savior of all the world* (1 John 4:14). He was never exclusive in His relationships but socialized with a variety of people. The Bible shares interactions Jesus had with Jewish religious leaders, a Samaritan woman (He actually talked to a woman!), tax collectors, those who were disabled, demon-possessed, judged as sinners, and society's second-class or devalued individuals such as widows, lepers, and children. Jesus was comfortable with every person He encountered.

While on the earth, Jesus demonstrated His love for every person because He desired to dance with every individual. The *invitation to dance with Him* was extended to all. Jesus came to save *all* the world and *at His name every knee will bow and every tongue will acknowledge that He is Lord* (Philippians 2:9-11).

From Grace to Grace:

Just as Jesus was inclusive and offered *Grace* to all individuals—even those considered different or *less than* by societal and cultural standards—you become a more well-rounded dancer and individual when you surround yourself with a variety of people, attempting to understand their background and culture.

And just as Jesus was comfortable with every person He encountered, we are encouraged to share God's *Grace* and Love with all, regardless of their ethnicity, socioeconomic background or circumstances.

Do you look for opportunities to meet and interact with individuals who are different from you? How can you show appreciation and value for every person you meet?

A dance community is formed.

On the Dance Floor:

Stepping into a dance studio for the first time can be both anxiety-producing and also liberating. It can be viewed as a place for a fresh start, where no one knows your name or history. A person begins the journey with a desire to begin a new chapter in his or her life, specifically through the experience of dance.

Some individuals begin dance lessons with a life partner, but more commonly, a person joins a studio as an individual. Many students are looking for a community of new friends; others might see time in the dance studio as a respite from the numerous roles and responsibilities they have. Personally, I enjoyed the freedom to have *solo* time to pursue my interest in dance. During the precious time of each lesson, I felt supported by instructors who solely focused on *my* growth and success.

Because of the shared experiences in the studio, a community formed, and students provided encouragement and support through injuries, setbacks, or life's challenges.

Dancing with Jesus:

When we begin our *dance with Jesus*, we are introduced to others who have become followers of Jesus by believing in Him as Savior. Their transformation process has also begun, and we share common experiences as parts of the Body of Christ.

As believers and followers, we share the same *dance floor* and common challenges. We can *encourage one another and build each other up* (1 Thessalonians 5:11). There are numerous reminders to *live a life worthy of the calling we have received by being completely humble, gentle and patiently bearing with one another in love* (Ephesians 4:1-2).

May the God who gives endurance and encouragement give you the same attitude of mind toward each other that Christ Jesus had (Romans 15:5).

From Grace to Grace:

Just as the dance community encourages each other, we should celebrate individual journeys and successes that come with our shared experiences.

Because you know how impactful it is to receive encouragement through life's ups and downs, you are able to empathetically support your family and friends during their journey. Though you may not understand their unique path, you can attempt to *graciously* love them while dancing within a community.

Every person is unique and special.

On the Dance Floor:

Every person on the dance floor is treated with equal individuality. The instructors made *me* feel like *I* was their favorite. Their undivided focus was only on *me* during *my* lesson. The instructor was fully present and in tune with *my* specific needs. I knew the instructor's goal was to help *me* be successful.

When I watched lessons from the sidelines, I noticed the same level of intentional focus—every student was also treated as a *favorite*. One of my first instructors, Christopher, mastered how to be fully focused and present with every student. He was intuitive, listening for cues and inquiring as to how she was feeling, thus making her feel unique and special.

Dancing with Jesus:

Each of us is uniquely remarkable and wonderfully made, with God's purposes and plans for our lives established before birth (Psalm 139:13-16). And each of us is uniquely seen and known by *the God who sees Me* (Genesis 16:13).

The invitation to *dance with Jesus* is inclusive and personal, *for the grace of God has appeared that offers salvation to all people* (Titus 2:11).

But *God does not show favoritism* as humans do (Acts 10:34; Romans 2:11). Skeptics of Jesus knew that *He did not show partiality but taught truthfully* (Luke 20:21). He truthfully sees every person as unique and special, not valuing one more than another.

From Grace to Grace:

When you understand and feel secure in your identity as a uniquely created individual who is seen, known, valued, and loved for your own self, you can extend that same viewpoint to every individual.

As you try to put yourself into the shoes of a person and understand his or her journey, you are better able to see, know, value, and love each person for who he or she is in God's eyes. There is no comparison, just admiration and appreciation for each person's unique journey.

Because God does not show favoritism, you can learn not to esteem anyone more highly than another but to treat every person with equal respect. It is an act of *grace* to show an individual that he or she is seen. You can do that with a smile or through a word of encouragement that communicates that they are seen and valued by you and, more importantly, by God.

I love watching you dance.

On the Dance Floor:

This phrase was spoken to me by a random woman at my first competition. Though considered a Newcomer, somehow I had inspired her, a beginning dancer, to continue her lessons. We learned each other's names and would run into each other at the various competitions, encouraging each other from the sidelines.

Interestingly, her acknowledgment of my presence on the dance floor and affirmation of my impact on her encouraged me to continue my journey.

My parents (who are seated in the foreground of this photo) rarely were able to watch me perform, but they were my biggest fans because they loved to watch me dance.

Dancing with Jesus:

Mary of Bethany inspires me. I love watching her *dance with Jesus*, choosing to sit at His feet to learn from Him. She expressed beautiful devotion to Him during the final days of His life.

Six days before the beginning of Jesus' final journey to the cross, His friend Mary poured very expensive perfume on His head during dinner. The disciples were indignant and accused her of extravagance.

Jesus affirmed her pure motives by responding, *Why are you bothering this woman? She has done a beautiful thing to me. The poor you will always have with you, but you will not always have me. She did what she could. When she poured this perfume on my body, she did it to prepare me for burial. Truly I tell you, wherever this gospel is preached throughout the world, what she has done will also be told, in memory of her* (Matthew 26:6-13, Mark 14:6-9, John 12:1-8).

Mary of Bethany's intimacy with Jesus inspires me to deepen my relationship with Him. I'm confident that He affirms my choice to sit and learn from Him. Though I am not in close proximity to Jesus as Mary was, beautiful intimacy is also possible for me because of my intentional *dance with Him*.

From Grace to Grace:

People inspire us with their acts of strength, beauty, and when serving others. Many acts of sacrifice or heroism are seen and known publicly. But most acts of service go unnoticed or unrecognized.

It is helpful to let individuals know that their actions (whether publicly seen or more privately noticed) have inspired them in specific ways. These unsung heroes probably are unaware of the impact they have made on your life, but your acknowledgment and affirmation can become a source of encouragement for them to continue their journey.

Welcome back!

On the Dance Floor:

Welcome back! All action stopped when a former student walked through the door. Instructors ran over to the returning student and enthusiastically gave the person a hug. I'd ask, *Who is that?*

Usually, the story of a person's return included the reason the student took a dance break: a physical injury, financial difficulty, change in job, or conflicting schedule. For many former students, the tug to resume dance lessons and rejoin the dance community brought them back to the studio and they were welcomed with open arms and celebration when they returned.

Dancing with Jesus:

During our dance with Jesus, sometimes (and for a variety of reasons), we take a *break* from the partnership. At times, we may sit on the sidelines and watch. Sometimes, we leave the dance floor altogether. But Jesus, always the *Gracious* gentleman, watches and waits. He understands the reasons we feel we might need a break. Maybe we have been hurt by the *spiritual dance community* (the church), or we are tired or injured.

Maybe we refuse to trust the partnership and leading of Jesus, deciding instead to go solo. Many know the story Jesus told of the son who walked away from his father and home but relented and returned. The father had been waiting and hosted a joyous return party. *We had to celebrate . . . he was dead and is alive again; he was lost and is found* (Luke 15:11-32).

Just like the Father who waited for His wayward son to return, Jesus waits for us to step onto the dance floor and resume the partnership. *Welcome back, let's celebrate! Will you dance with Me—again?*

From Grace to Grace:

Occasionally, relationships are accompanied by strains, breaks, and time periods of emotional distance or going solo. Though imperfect ourselves—and most likely a contributor to drama within a relationship—if you adopt the *gracious* attitude of watching, waiting, expecting, and praying for reconciliation, there is a celebration when the relationship is restored!

Is there anyone you need to encourage to begin dancing within a relationship again?

BRONZE LEVEL

After the initial exposure to the ballroom dance experience, a student is asked what level of involvement he or she is interested in. Though many students take lessons for social reasons, they are quickly introduced to opportunities to demonstrate their new skills by performing (gulp!) in an encouraging studio setting.

Based on a person's level of interest, some students begin to progress through a specific dance curriculum and schedule consistent lessons with an instructor. The student determines which dance styles to focus on and begins laying down a foundation of steps and patterns.

Some dancers enjoy the competitive aspect of ballroom dance and begin their path toward showcasing their dance journey before a panel of judges. Others choose to perform theatrical routines for an audience. Whatever path a person chooses is specific to the individual and involves challenges and accomplishments.

This next section of phrases provides a representation of my dance journey through the Bronze Level. No longer a Newcomer, I intentionally focused on learning the dance curriculum. Steps and patterns progressed from the *closed* position to dancing side-by-side in the *open* position, holding one hand of my partner. Occasionally, both hands were released and I learned to briefly dance independently.

Because I decided that my dance journey would not be limited primarily to social settings, I started to prepare to perform in local competitions. I was introduced to a new world of the ballroom dance scene and purchased my first shimmering ballroom dress. I was also exposed to professional hair stylists and make-up artists who were trained to make me look my best on the competitive dance floor. Fun fact: I wore false eyelashes for the first time in my life.

Welcome to Bronze Level and the fascinating world of ballroom dance competition!

Strength and beauty

On the Dance Floor:

The man presents the frame with strength so that the woman's beauty can be showcased. Because there are different roles for males and females, there are different visual presentations. A man's suit, typically black, accentuates the strength of his frame. The woman showcases her beauty with a colorful dress adorned with jewels that draw attention to and accentuate her beauty.

My instructor Christopher's comment *You are a very beautiful woman* profoundly impacted me. I knew he used the word *beautiful* to imply more than my dancing or physical beauty. He meant that I, myself, my presence, was beautiful. Because feminine beauty is showcased and featured in ballroom dance, I felt affirmed and encouraged to be beautiful, to be graceful, and to inspire others to be beautiful on and off the dance floor.

Dancing with Jesus:

We are *made in the image of God*, both *male and female* (Genesis 1:27). When admiring the variety of creatures and intricacies of flowers and nature scenes, we are amazed by the *beauty*, color, and symmetry that reflects a creative God who is *beautiful*. There is also a *wildness* in nature—a *strength* that is also an aspect of the image of God. So, when we see a strong male and beautiful female dancing in partnership, we are witnessing God's created attributes of Strength AND Beauty.

I heard God say two things: 'I am powerful, and I am very kind' (Psalm 62:11-12 CEV).

We are made in God's image and reflect both Strength AND Beauty. Jesus was both strong AND beautiful. One of my favorite authors, John Eldredge, describes Jesus as a *Beautiful Outlaw*. Jesus was physically strong, protective, and zealously standing up for justice.

AND Jesus was gentle, offering compassionate and supportive strength. Jesus' strength was founded on the beautiful motive of Love. He was empathetic and tender AND displayed confidence and authority that conveyed strength. As we progress through our life's *dance with Jesus*, we will begin to take on both aspects of Jesus—His strength AND His beauty.

From Grace to Grace:

The following statements may be simplifications and generalizations, but this is what I have observed from the dance world: We need both men AND women to dance completely. Beauty softens Strength. Strength emboldens Beauty. A man's strength is complete when it is complemented with gentleness and compassion. A woman's beauty is more compelling when complemented with confidence and inner strength of character.

We should be encouraged to develop both aspects of Strength AND Beauty in our personal lives. Even as women who were created to be beautiful, we understand that strength accompanies beauty. And a man will learn that just as with Jesus, there is beauty and compassion within strength. You can affirm these qualities in others and encourage each other to be the best version of *strong* AND *beautiful* that God intended.

Establish a solid foundation.

On the Dance Floor:

During the early stages of my dance lessons, I wanted to quickly learn the steps and progress through the levels. But I soon learned to appreciate a slower pace of learning. If foundational layers are missed by rushing through the levels, I would need to backtrack to the basics, and eventually, the quality of my dancing would suffer. As I progressed to higher skill levels, I would continue to attend group classes to review and strengthen the foundational aspects of my dancing, such as frame, foot position, and connections.

I learned to take time to review foundational basics: steps, patterns, technique, and posture. Though it seemed more exciting to advance quickly, I was reminded not to rush the process. There are no shortcuts to a successful end result. It was appealing to hurry up the process to do the fancy steps or tricks, but a lack of foundational skills, strength, and proper body position would not achieve the desired outcome of dancing beautifully.

Dancing with Jesus:

The foundation of our lives is built on the Rock—Jesus. We cannot rush ahead of Him. Our relationship with Jesus requires action and practice. Stepping on the dance floor with Jesus is the first step, but incomplete. We must take the time to set the proper foundation so that the relationship we build with Jesus will hold firmly for eternity.

Why do you call Me 'Lord, Lord,' and don't do the things I say? I will show you what someone is like who comes to Me, hears My words, and acts on them: He is like a man building a house who dug deep and laid the foundation on the rock. When the flood came, the river crashed against that house and couldn't shake it because it was well-built. But the one who hears and does not act is like a man who built a house on the ground without a foundation. The river crashed against it, and immediately it collapsed. And the destruction of that house was great! (Luke 6:46-49).

By the grace God has given me, I laid a foundation as a wise builder, and someone else is building on it. But each one should build with care (1 Corinthians 3:10).

From Grace to Grace:

Foundations in all areas of life are important. Establishing foundational communication patterns are critical in relationships. It has been said that *slow and steady wins the race*. It takes time to establish a relationship, build a career, or achieve a goal.

As I used to tell my kids, *Take the time to do it right.* Rushing ahead through a project or learning experience commonly requires having to undo part of it or repeat a section because quality suffers.

Foundations are important, so build intentionally with care. What foundations are important in your life? Do some of these foundations need to be bolstered or reinforced?

The frame provides safety and freedom.

On the Dance Floor:

There is comfort, safety, and freedom within the boundaries of the frame. Even when letting go of my partner's hand and dancing independently, there is safety and comfort in knowing the frame, my Leader, is still there to come back to.

We learn to trust that the Leader and the frame will be there—no matter what.

Dancing with Jesus:

Jesus said that *He will never leave us nor forsake us* (Hebrews 13:5). Even as we grow and are released to dance and minister more independently, He is always there to encourage and comfort us.

For I am convinced that neither death nor life, neither angels nor demons, neither the present nor the future, nor any powers, neither height nor depth, nor anything else in all creation, will be able to separate us from the love of God that is in Christ Jesus our Lord (Romans 8:38-39).

We know that Jesus' intent behind the boundaries of His frame comes from a place of Love and perfect intent. The Lord takes hold of our right hand, strengthens us and says not to fear because He will help us (Isaiah 41:10, 13-14).

From Grace to Grace:

A child feels safe within loving boundaries. When parenting, the framework of unconditional love and family boundaries are established for the safety of the child. God's boundaries—motivated by His frame of Love—also need to be taught to children.

Within those parameters of love, a child senses the freedom to explore. As the child grows and learns self-control, boundaries are lessened because a parent knows the foundations have been laid, and the child understands the intent of the parameters that were provided.

Where can you demonstrate loving *grace* by creating boundaries that provide safety and freedom?

You are a dancer.

On the Dance Floor:

When I looked across the room, even if I didn't know you, I could tell that you are a dancer by the way you walk and carry yourself.

This statement from my instructor, Kyle, encouraged me to continue with my dance journey even when I didn't believe it myself or was able to confidently say, *I'm a dancer!*

You are a dancer . . . it is in you . . . our goal is to uncover the dancer in you. It is a process, but you are a dancer. It will just take some time to peel away the layers that are hiding who you truly are.

My instructors probably had no idea how profound these words were, and I started focusing on the process of *peeling away the layers* to reveal the dancer in me.

Dancing with Jesus:

We are made in the image of God. He knows how we have been created and what our gifts and talents are. The more we trust in who He says we are, as seen through His eyes, the clearer our commitment to trust the process of transforming us into who He has created us to become.

Even before Jesus' friend Peter understood his potential, Jesus spoke to Peter of an identity that he would grow into (Matthew 16:17-19).

As we spend time with Jesus, dancing with Him, allowing Him to transform us by His Spirit, we reflect His likeness and His glory (2 Corinthians 3:18). And we become more of a reflection of who He created us to be.

From Grace to Grace:

Many people carry with them a false identity of who they are in God's eyes because of the lies that have been spoken about them. These lies include the following phrases: *You don't matter. You're not enough. You're too much. You're a disappointment. You will never measure up.*

When you begin to speak to a person the truth of their identity in Jesus, untruths are revealed and lies begin to peel away. The truth of a person's identity, as seen through God's eyes, is revealed.

It might take a person time to accept the revelation of who they are based on truth, but in time, they, too, will see themselves through the eyes of Jesus—loved, valued, beautiful, strong, with unique gifts and talents are given to them by God to be used for His purposes and for His glory.

Instructors personalize a student's learning plan.

On the Dance Floor:

Every student learns differently and at an individual rate. Even though each of my instructors had his or her own personality and style of teaching based on their own experiences, they adjusted their instruction to how I processed and learned a new concept or step.

Because one of my instructors was aware of my journey with Jesus, sometimes he used analogies based on Biblical stories. Instead of saying, *Hold your arms in an oval shape*, he provided a visual for me: *Shape your arms as if you are Martha holding a platter while serving Jesus.*

Though teaching methods and strategies were different, the instructors had a common goal—my successful progress as a dancer. They adjusted their teaching to best facilitate how I learn.

Dancing with Jesus:

While on earth Jesus interacted with groups and also personally with individuals. He spoke differently with women than with men. There were numerous times when He was more direct, even confrontational when speaking with men. His interactions with women typically were more tender and gentler, and He addressed their specific physical and emotional needs.

Jesus used analogies and spoke in parables. He commonly asked questions, engaging a person's intellect instead of just giving information. Jesus provided hands-on opportunities for His disciples to serve by assisting in feeding the crowd of five thousand (John 6:1-13) and healing the sick (Mark 6:7-12).

Jesus knows us intimately and uses specific methods with every one of us to facilitate our individual growth. He knows us best, and we can trust that His teaching methods and His will are perfectly aligned with how we learn and grow.

From Grace to Grace:

Because each individual has different learning styles and a unique journey, it is helpful to put yourself into the shoes of another person and see his or her viewpoint. Then, you can personalize communication based on that individual's personality, learning style, strengths, or sensibilities.

When you *love your neighbor as yourself*, you can attempt to interact with each person in a way he or she will understand and relate to—not just how *you* might prefer or what you feel comfortable with. *Grace* humbly seeks to love another the way that person wants to be loved. By focusing on a person's learning style, you will have more connection with that individual's growth journey.

Can you describe the learning styles of those in your sphere? How can you best adapt your interactions to facilitate their growth?

Get out of your head.

On the Dance Floor:

On numerous occasions, my instructors would encourage me to *get out of my head*, follow and trust the leaders, and listen more to my body and heart. When I was intensely focused on trying to do the right thing or analyzing what went wrong, I lost the purpose of why I was there—which was to learn to dance freely.

When dancing from the *head*, there is a lack of confidence; dancing feels contrived, and it doesn't flow naturally. Many times, I anticipated or tried to pre-think what the leader was going to do. That usually got me into trouble because I wasn't completely following the Leader.

Over time, I began to listen to the music and trust that my heart would connect to my Leader and the steps that were foundationally in my muscle memory would flow freely.

Dancing with Jesus:

Head knowledge is important but knowing Jesus as our Leader is a relationship that comes from the heart. I might know lots of details *about* Jesus, but knowledge *about* Him does not necessarily create a relationship.

You study the Scriptures diligently because you think that in them you have eternal life. These are the very Scriptures that testify about Me (John 5:39).

Only when I confessed to Jesus that I didn't really know Him relationally and asked to experience His heart and His motives could I dance relationally with Him, trusting in His lead while listening to the music of our connected hearts?

From Grace to Grace:

You can know a lot of details about a person's story (head knowledge), but until you begin to understand his or her story from the perspective of his or her heart, motives and viewpoint, it is not a true relationship.

When you approach life and relationships primarily from the *head* it means you move through life with the perspective of analyzing others, with a sense of duty or obligation towards others. These contrived relationships can be somewhat stunted and certainly not freely expressed.

But when you learn to live from a *heart* that reflects the *Grace* of Jesus, you dance through life more naturally, authentically, and freely.

Dance is simple, but it's not easy.

On the Dance Floor:

The initial phase of my ballroom dance journey felt relatively simple because I had previous exposure to dance movement, related musically and was fairly coordinated. I caught on quickly to the basics of ballroom dance but soon realized that to be a good dancer, there were layers upon layers of technical nuances and complexities that I had to learn.

At times, when parked outside the studio, knowing my lesson would not be easy, I had to gather courage and tell myself that it was worth the stretching and growth to reach my goal. The beginning levels were simple, but to dance beautifully and fully like I knew my heart wanted to would take consistent and persistent effort.

Usually at this phase of the dance journey, a person begins to prioritize his or her interest level and to what level of skill he or she would like to achieve. Many students are content with the basics of social dance and prefer not to progress to the higher levels of dance technique. Because I chose to dance more than socially, I realized there were increasing levels of involvement requiring time, financial commitment to lessons, and emotional investment.

Dancing with Jesus:

The introduction to *dancing with Jesus* may seem simple. It really is! *Repent and believe* (Mark 1:15). The next steps show that *dancing with Jesus*, though simple (requiring belief and faith in Him), is definitely not easy. There is suffering, discouragement, and persecution. But we must press on.

Listen then to what the parable of the sower means: When anyone hears the message about the kingdom and does not understand it, the evil one comes and snatches away what was sown in their heart. This is the seed sown along the path. The seed falling on rocky ground refers to someone who hears the word and at once receives it with joy. But since they have no roots, they last only a short time. When trouble or persecution comes because of the word, they quickly fall away. The seed falling among the thorns refers to someone who hears the word, but the worries of this life and the deceitfulness of wealth choke the word, making it unfruitful. But the seed falling on good soil refers to someone who hears the word and understands it. This is the one who produces a crop, yielding a hundred, sixty or thirty times what was sown (Matthew 13:18-23).

What is required after a simple commitment to the dance with Jesus? Jesus said to His disciples that *whoever wants to be My disciple must deny themselves and take up their cross and follow Me* (Matthew 16:24).

Denying oneself and taking up my cross is not easy, but the eternal rewards will be worth all the challenges.

From Grace to Grace:

Like most things in life, the road to success, victory, or accomplishment is not an easy one. But the desire of our hearts compels us forward through the challenges requiring *blood, sweat, and tears*. We discover that what may initially be seen as simple takes more than an initial interest in an activity. Determination and passion are required to push through what will inevitably come—struggles and setbacks.

You can encourage others when they are faced with obstacles by reminding them to persist. Holding on to the hope of the desired outcome will help a person through the aspects that are *not easy*.

You are dancing beautifully right where you are.

On the Dance Floor:

After expressing frustration with my perceived lack of progress while wistfully wishing I were dancing at a higher level, Kyle spoke the encouraging and *grace*-filled phrase, *You are dancing beautifully right where you are.* The atmosphere in the studio was one of acceptance for the personal journey of each of us.

Accolades for personal growth milestones were equally given to beginning and more experienced students. The instructors were trained to give positive feedback and encouragement. Because all the instructors were simultaneously receiving personal coaching for their professional development, they were acknowledging that they too, were growing and not to be wistfully wishing to be farther along in their journey.

I consistently received encouragement and *grace* from the instructors and was reminded to give *grace* to myself. There was no rush to get there (wherever *there* is) faster. Dance is a journey. Be patient with the process and enjoy right where you are because *you are dancing beautifully.*

Dancing with Jesus:

Jesus' friend Mary of Bethany was scolded by others for what they deemed inappropriate. She looked to Jesus for His approval. He affirmed that she was *dancing beautifully just where she was*. And He valued her beautiful expression of devotion.

Leave her alone, said Jesus. *Why are you bothering her? She has done a beautiful thing to me . . . She did what she could* (Mark 14:6-9).

Jesus does not compare us with others. If we are dancing with Him, we are doing the best we can right where we are. We are *dancing beautifully* with Him. Yes, we are not where we eventually want to be and continue to show our weaknesses and failings (sin), but we are reminded to be patient, trust our Leader, and keep dancing with Him.

From Grace to Grace:

Receiving *grace* during the process of your journey transforms the way you relate to family members and friends. Remind yourself that your loved ones are also on a growth journey and *dancing beautifully right where they are*. It is mutually freeing to create a *grace*-filled environment that is non-judgmental, patient, and encouraging and does not compare individual journeys but is unconditionally loving.

Extending *grace* does not guarantee non-stressful relationships or take away challenges. But just as God gives us time to grow and be transformed by His *Grace*, you too can provide *grace* for your relationships to flourish by recognizing that each individual has a unique dance journey with Jesus.

Who do you need to extend *grace* to by reminding yourself that he or she is dancing beautifully right where they are?

Trust the instructors and follow their example.

On the Dance Floor:

When I watched my instructors perform or compete, my trust in their coaching expertise increased. Though they were receiving private coaching at the professional level, when the instructors gave lessons in the dance studio, they willingly adapted to and danced at my amateur level. They humbly remembered what it was like to be in my amateur shoes even as they were simultaneously competing as pros.

Instead of being condescending or impatient with my progress, my pro coach Kyle used to say, *This is the way I would do it* or, *This is the way I learned to do it.* He provided an example for me to emulate and follow.

Dancing with Jesus:

Jesus knows what it is like to be in our shoes because He lived in human reality. He can relate to our human experience, and we can trust that He understands because He walked a similar journey.

God's will is that we are conformed to the image of Jesus because He is the firstborn among many to follow (Romans 8:29). Jesus humbled Himself and came from heaven to earth in the likeness of a man, experiencing our reality of humanity and learning through obedience (Philippians 2:5-8).

We also learn from other followers of Jesus. The Apostle Paul—master student and teacher—encouraged the followers of Jesus to *follow my example, as I follow Christ* (1 Corinthians 11:1).

Therefore we also, since we are surrounded by so great a cloud of witnesses, let us lay aside every weight, and the sin which so easily ensnares us, and let us run with endurance the race that is set before us, looking unto Jesus, the author and finisher of our faith, who for the joy that was set before Him endured the cross, despising the shame, and has sat down at the right hand of the throne of God (Hebrews 12:1-2).

From Grace to Grace:

You give *grace* to others by recognizing each person is on his or her own journey. You look at those who are more experienced to learn from their life and faith journeys. And when others look to you as a mentor, you can *graciously* remember your path and humbly share what you have learned. Encourage others to keep moving forward through the challenges and difficulties that invariably will present themselves along the way.

Keep learning and growing while sharing *grace* within your everyday life and modeling what it looks like to value continual transformation into the likeness of Jesus.

I believe in you more than you do.

On the Dance Floor:

I believe in you more than you because I see what you are capable of. At the beginning of my journey, when moments of doubt set in, Serge encouraged me with that statement. He knew that if I didn't give up but kept moving forward toward my goal, I, too, would begin to understand what I was capable of. I learned to trust my instructors to stretch, grow, and transform me. They could see what I was capable of based on my physical ability, musicality, and heart's desire.

Serge wisely cautioned me against watching videos of my dance performances, knowing it could be discouraging because I might tend to see my weaknesses instead of my progress. Because my instructors believed in me (even more than I did), I improved during every dance session.

Dancing with Jesus:

Jesus knew what Peter was capable of and could look past Peter's inadequacies to see how his strengths and weaknesses would eventually be used for powerful Kingdom purposes.

Even after Peter's denial of Jesus during His trial, Jesus restored the relationship after His resurrection, essentially saying to Peter, *I believe in you. Go feed My sheep* (John 21:15-17).

From Grace to Grace:

We are grateful for those who speak about our potential and encourage us in our growth journey. By their example we learn to extend that *grace* to others.

Grace believes in people. *Grace* smiles through their inadequacies. *Grace* sees people as Jesus sees them, even through incompleteness and shortcomings. A lifestyle of *grace* encourages others in their growth and speaks the truth about who they are becoming. The presence of *grace* encourages others to keep taking the next step forward, even when they don't believe in themselves.

Look expectantly for a person in your path who might need a sweet gift of *grace* today. Then, watch the expression on their face change when they are affirmed by your *gracious* words.

I see your potential.

On the Dance Floor:

Many times during my lessons, I shared the details of my life journey with my instructors. I found myself describing who I was—timid, shy, and cautious—partly to explain some of my shortcomings and also to give my instructors permission to stretch and grow me out of what I described as my personality.

There were times when I felt that I was actually bravely conquering fears. But I continued to fall back into the explanation of who I thought I was instead of speaking the truth of who I was becoming by facing and conquering my self-perception of timidity.

On one occasion, Kyle responded, *That's not how I see you. I see your potential.* Similar to the previous statement regarding believing in a person, Kyle stated it another way, affirming that he saw my *potential* as a dancer. I didn't see it clearly yet, but he did.

There is a tendency to be discouraged in the growth process. I learned to trust the professional's viewpoint, not my own, because he saw *potential*. So, I stopped explaining (making excuses) the way I saw myself and started telling myself that I was brave, I was conquering fears and I was no longer afraid to dance in front of others. I started seeing my *potential* as seen through my instructor's eyes.

Dancing with Jesus:

Jesus saw individuals through the eyes of *Grace*, seeing their potential. On one occasion Nathanael was so impacted by Jesus' knowledge of his deepest identity that he proclaimed Jesus was the Son of God (John 1:43-49).

When Jesus saw a crippled woman, He called her forward and healed her. By calling her a *daughter of Abraham* (Luke 13:16), Jesus elevated her social status with a tender reference of inclusion. She probably didn't see herself as a *daughter of Abraham*. Certainly, others didn't, but Jesus called her that because that was who she was in His eyes.

The Father sees us as His children. Because we are in Christ, He sees us through the lens of His Son, Jesus.

Yet to all who did receive him, to those who believed in his name, he gave the right to become children of God (John 1:12).

So in Christ Jesus you are all children of God through faith (Galatians 3:26).

And God raised us up with Christ and seated us with him in the heavenly realms in Christ Jesus (Ephesians 2:6). He sees us as forgiven, raised up and seated in the heavenly realms. I'm learning to trust how God sees me in Christ.

From Grace to Grace:

Grace affirms a person's potential when you tell them, *I see who you are becoming, and it is beautiful and strong. You are growing into who God created you to be.*

Grace reminds people that their identity is in who Jesus says he or she is, not who the world says or what the individual believes about themself. *Grace* speaks the truth of who they are in God's eyes —a child of God, made in the image of God, being transformed into the likeness of Christ by choosing to continue to *dance with Jesus*.

Don't compare your dance journey with another person.

On the Dance Floor:

Every person is on his or her unique dance journey. We come into the studio with individual needs, desires, and goals. Progress within an individual's dance program depends on the investment of time and finances, a person's physical ability, and musicality.

On a human level, we can have a tendency to be jealous of a fellow dancer who dances at a higher level. We may become discouraged because we are not as skilled. But we forget that each person has been dancing his or her own path and that our journey inherently looks different because we are unique individuals. Once we establish the mindset of not comparing ourselves with another, we are freed to continue on our path and can celebrate and encourage fellow students. We all have the same goal—to become better dancers. Remember, each person is *dancing beautifully right where they are.*

Dancing with Jesus:

It is not wise to compare ourselves with others (2 Corinthians 10:12) or *think more highly of ourselves* (Romans 12:3). We are reminded to *esteem others highly* (Philippians 2:3) and *remain humble before God, so that He may exalt us. We cast our cares on Him because He cares for us personally* (1 Peter 5:6-7).

While becoming acquainted with the various stories of how Jesus interacted with individuals, I observed how He met each person uniquely, based on his or her specific needs and circumstances. Jesus adapted His style of communication to each person.

Jesus had an intriguing dialogue with Peter that has impacted how I view people and their individual stories. When Jesus told Peter how his life journey would end, Peter looked at the disciple John and inquired about John's story. Jesus responded by implying that John's journey was not Peter's concern and that instead, Peter should focus on following Jesus (John 21:20-23).

From Grace to Grace:

One of the greatest gifts a child can be given is to know that he or she is loved by God and by a community of family and friends that celebrates each individual. When you embrace the truth that every person is loved for whom he or she uniquely is in God's eyes, you will foster confidence that comes from an identity that is not based on comparing with another person. You will choose to see each person through the lens of God's Love and *Grace*.

It is commonly accepted that each child is unique, with different personalities, interests, and talents. When working with children, not only do we attempt to individualize instruction, but we also teach them not to compare themselves with others because this is not wise and can have debilitating effects on their lives.

It may even be more difficult to give *grace* to ourselves as we relate to other adults. Is this a good reminder for you to cherish your own journey and not compare your life with another?

I choose to stretch and grow.

On the Dance Floor:

It was my choice to face and overcome challenges on the dance floor. It was my choice to pursue a growth path that included stretching my physical, emotional, and mental capacities. I knew there would be challenges, and I chose to face them.

It was my choice to face and conquer fears. The first fears I struggled with were the fear of being watched, of not being good enough, of making mistakes, and of being judged. These fears came from a performance-based filter established in my youth. I was determined to change this mindset, so I courageously shared my story and trusted my instructors to help me overcome whatever held me back from dancing freely.

I knew that in my heart, I had the capacity to dance the way I envisioned it. There *was* a dancer inside—I just needed someone to help peel away the *non-dancer* layers and fears and lay down new foundational skills and techniques. I realized that my physicality was diminishing with age and that every day was a gift.

So, I continued to step onto the dance floor and chose courageously to grow, knowing it would take time, effort, and money. I committed to the process of facing emotional fears and stretching beyond the limitations of my entrenched personality of timidity. The choice was clear: Do I want to face fears or limp through life being less than who God created me to be? *I choose to stretch and grow.*

Dancing with Jesus:

Jesus asked a man who had been disabled for thirty-eight years an astounding question: *Do you want to get well?* (John 5:1-15). By asking this question, the individual was abruptly confronted with reality. What were the obstacles to getting well? How intensely was his desire to get well? Jesus knew He would take care of the initial obstacle, but what changes might be required if he were healed? Jesus listened and then healed the man.

Jesus never forces Himself on a person or prods a person to grow. We have free will, but He graciously asks, *Do you want to get well?* Jesus is more than willing to assist us on our journey of restoration and wholeness, but the choice is ours.

I sensed Jesus asking me, *Do you want to conquer your fears? Would you like to overcome your timidity?* Yes, I want to conquer my fears and dance freely and fully. Yes, I want to conquer my people-pleasing tendency. I trust You, Jesus. Heal, restore, empower. I choose to trust You!

From Grace to Grace:

Any growth journey is *your* growth journey. You are only responsible for *yourself,* not for another person's journey. You cannot force another person to change or will a desire of heart onto another person. The role *grace* plays in your relationship with others is to encourage and celebrate another person's journey of growth.

As you courageously choose to face and conquer fears with Jesus' help, you might also be a source of encouragement for others to face and conquer their fears.

Correction and critique benefit my growth.

On the Dance Floor:

My previous background of performance-based evaluation, people-pleasing, and fear of disappointing an authority figure created sensitivity to receiving correction. At the beginning of my dance journey, sometimes I would sit in the parking lot, take a deep breath, and muster the courage to go into the studio, knowing I would be stretched and challenged. And corrected.

I knew that correction would come with dance lessons, but it took a while to feel comfortable with the continual critique. Essentially, the entire lesson (with the exception of small talk) consisted of instruction, corrections, tweaks, practice, and adjustments. But because the environment of *grace* had been established, it wasn't long before correction was a natural reality and I didn't fear it.

I chose to continue with lessons, realizing that evaluation and correction were given for the purpose of my growth. The environment of *grace* in the dance studio, with abundant patience and encouragement, changed the dynamic of correction.

Correction was *graciously* given, not because the instructor was upset with me or even disappointed with me. Correction helped my growth and was always accompanied by accolades, affirmation, and celebration. Instructors would gush, *That's it! You did that beautifully*! *Yes, that looks great! Wonderful job! I'm proud of you!* Once I understood the *purpose* of the instructional correction, I actually began to value the comments.

Dancing with Jesus:

Jesus came full of *Grace* AND Truth. *The Word became flesh and made his dwelling among us. We have seen his glory, the glory of the one and only Son, who came from the Father, full of grace and truth* (John 1:14).

When correction (Truth) is given within a framework of Love and patience (*Grace*), the motive can be trusted. I'm reminded that correction is for *my* benefit. *The Father corrects and disciplines those He loves* (Proverbs 3:12, Hebrews 12:6). *Jesus does not condemn* (John 3:17) but speaks truth with *Grace*.

There is no fear in love (1 John 4:18). Gracious correction is not associated with punishment but with growth. When I believed that the transformation process of growing into God's image was not only facilitated by Jesus but done from the perspective of His *Grace,* I could embrace His truth. He sees and knows my potential, and in His Love, He is the One who transforms me.

Jesus is *for* me. He is growing me into a more beautiful dancer. I can trust Him and His truth—including His correction and discipline—because He offers *Grace* in Love.

From Grace to Grace:

When you have experienced *grace*—whether on the human level or from Jesus—and understand and trust the motives underlying correction, you can extend the same *graciousness* to others. Truth spoken, even in the form of correction, comes from a foundation of love.

Truth graciously spoken in love (Ephesians 4:15) is more readily received. It may take the recipient of instructional correction time to trust and respond, but as he or she learns to trust the loving motive of the communication, the benefit is growth.

I'm proud of you.

On the Dance Floor:

The dance journey, though fun, takes hard work to improve and grow. Because I chose to continue to progress through the higher levels of dance, there were many times when I lost sight of how drastically I had developed as a dancer since stepping into the studio that first day. It was also difficult to quantify the degree to which I had overcome my fears.

One of the most gracious comments that served to bolster my courage to continue was spoken by Kyle. *You have worked so hard and come such a long way since you began. I'm proud of you.*

Dancing with Jesus:

We make a choice to follow Jesus and to grow into His image. We also recognize there are rewards available to those who follow Jesus and are faithful to the talents given to them.

Jesus told the example of servants who developed the talents given to them. *So he who had received five talents came and brought five other talents, saying, 'Lord, you delivered to me five talents; look, I have gained five more talents besides them.' His lord said to him, 'Well done, good and faithful servant; you were faithful over a few things, I will make you ruler over many things. Enter into the joy of your lord.' He also who had received two talents came and said, 'Lord, you delivered to me two talents; look, I have gained two more talents besides them.' His lord said to him, 'Well done, good and faithful servant; you have been faithful over a few things, I will make you ruler over many things. Enter into the joy of your lord'* (Matthew 25:20-23).

We are reminded that individual rewards are based on individual talent given and how a person develops and manages that gift. Affirmation of a job *well done* is a gift, and one day, I look forward to hearing that phrase spoken by Jesus.

From Grace to Grace:

Any journey of growth is challenging. Every person longs to be affirmed for the diligence and effort they invest in a project. We all need to be reminded of the bigger perspective of progression which takes an investment of time.

There can be external rewards, such as good grades, a pay raise, or a promotion. But a spoken word of affirmation such as, *I'm proud of you and your hard work and the progress you have made* makes a huge impact in the heart of the recipient. *Grace* speaks *grace* to another.

Does the name of a person who might need to hear a word of affirmation come to mind?

Listen to me.

On the Dance Floor:

The dance partnership can be stressful, especially for those who choose the path of competition. More time and money are invested, and routines become increasingly complex and physically demanding.

During an escalating conversation between student and instructor, it was apparent that the instructor thought the student was stubbornly doing it her way: *You have tried it your way, now why don't you listen to me and try to do what I'm asking you to do?*

The implicit message from the instructor was: *Listen to me. Trust me. I'm the instructor, the master.*

Dancing with Jesus:

Imagine the powerful scene when Peter, James and John were with Jesus and a bright cloud covered them. A voice from the cloud said, *This is My Son, whom I love and am well pleased with. Listen to Him!* (Matthew 17:5, Mark 9:7).

John 10:1-4 describes Jesus as the Good Shepherd who tends the sheep. *My sheep listen to my voice; I know them, and they follow Me. I give them eternal life, and they shall never perish; no one will snatch them out of My hand* (John 10:27-28). The sheep listen to Him and follow Him because they know His voice.

I am the Way, the Truth and the Life (John 14:6). Why would we want to listen to or follow anyone other than Jesus?

Many times, we try to do it our way, forgetting that Jesus is perfect, knows perfectly, knows us perfectly and is *The Way*. Listen to Him, the Master. Trust Him and where He is taking you on your journey.

From Grace to Grace:

One of the most challenging conversations in any relationship relates to who is *right*. The parent-child relationship is a challenge because there is a balancing act of letting the child learn on his or her own while exploring learning options AND listening to and accepting the voice of authority and experience. There are times of instruction when the child must accept the authority of the parent and listen to the voice of experience.

You can give *grace* to those you interact with who might not be receptive to listening to your insights or well-meaning advice. Maybe it is a timing issue, and instead of becoming offended by the lack of valuing your input, offer *grace*.

More importantly, you can convey *grace* to another person by listening to their words and heart. Their opinions and viewpoints can be received with an attitude of *grace* even though you might not be in agreement with them.

Practice what is learned.

On the Dance Floor:

You may have heard that *practice makes perfect*. More importantly, that *perfect practice makes perfect.* It is important to lay down foundational layers, remembering not to rush the process. Then practice.

A student strives to train muscle memory so that a skill becomes a habit. When a new dance concept or step was initially introduced, I was asked to do it again and again and again. Because I practiced it three times in a row didn't mean I could reproduce the movement correctly, but the initial foundation in my muscle memory had been laid. It would still take additional practice to reinforce the skill until it became a habit.

Dancing with Jesus:

Though we know we cannot be perfect like our Father in heaven, perfecting holiness is a worthwhile goal and is an intentional process. *Become perfect as your heavenly Father is perfect* (Matthew 5:48).

Therefore, since we have these promises, dear friends, let us purify ourselves from everything that contaminates body and spirit, perfecting holiness out of reverence for God (2 Corinthians 7:1).

Our spiritual journey requires practicing what we have been taught. *Do what you have learned and received and heard and seen in me, and the God of peace will be with you* (Philippians 4:9).

From Grace to Grace:

Growth and transformation take time. Just as learning dance patterns takes practice and time, it takes time to lay down and establish helpful and positive life patterns. You are grateful when you are given *grace* and patience during your growth process so you can extend *grace* and patience to those within your relationships who are also in a growth process.

Just as it takes much time and practice (with missteps and falls) for a baby to learn to walk, you can remember to be patient with others during their journey, even when they have missteps or falls.

Be beautiful.

On the Dance Floor:

My instructor once said *I can either say, 'Hold your head up' or 'Be beautiful.' Which statement resonates more with you?*

The contrast between dancing from the head with acquired techniques (*hold your head up*) or dancing from the heart (*be beautiful*) might be subtle, but the implications are noteworthy. Interestingly, whenever Kyle would use the phrase *be beautiful,* not only did my head lift, but my entire body was energized; a smile came on my face, and there was an anticipation of dancing to the music.

Dancing with Jesus:

There are numerous Scriptural references to *beauty*, specifically describing the *beauty of the Lord* (Psalm 27:4, 90:17) and advising us to *worship the Lord in the beauty of holiness* (Psalm 29:2, 96:9).

Because beauty and holiness are qualities of Jesus—the Prince of Peace and King of kings—I aspire to reflect those qualities. As I continue to *dance with Jesus*, I'm encouraged to know that He is the One who clothes me with His beauty and the splendor of His holiness. Therefore, *The King will greatly desire your beauty. Because He is your Lord, worship Him* (Psalm 45:11).

From Grace to Grace:

When you see individuals from a perspective of what they are capable of (*though they don't believe it themselves*) or what potential they have (*though they might not see it*), you encourage them by affirming their beauty.

You might be tempted to focus on giving a person advice, tips, or suggestions to help with her or his success, but a deeper level of motivation, inspiration, and encouragement comes when you speak your belief in what a person is capable of and of his or her potential.

Speaking words of *grace* encourages an individual to live from the perspective of how God sees them. Your greatest gift is to introduce them to Jesus, the only One who perfectly sees and knows their potential of beauty and holiness made possible through Him.

You haven't learned it until you can do it yourself.

On the Dance Floor:

Even though ballroom dance requires a partner, there comes a point in learning where steps and patterns need to be performed by the individual. During the process of learning a specific syllabus of steps and patterns, an important component is when the student is required to *test out* and demonstrate that he or she can do the step without a partner. *Testing out* after each level ensures the dancer knows the steps, patterns, and technique.

This process of *doing it yourself* also applies to complex routines. Each person in the partnership should strive to learn the sequences individually so that he or she doesn't have to rely on his or her partner.

Dancing with Jesus:

Jesus sent His disciples out in partnerships of twos, giving them authority to represent Him. He was essentially giving them an opportunity to *practice* what they had learned from Him. They were given authority to drive out demons, cure diseases, and heal sick people (Mark 6:7-12; Luke 9:1-6).

On one occasion, when a crowd gathered to hear Jesus speak, there was no food. He told the disciples, *You find something for them to eat.* They did their best and gathered what was available—five loaves and two fish. Of course, feeding the crowd was humanly impossible, but Jesus used their humble attempt and performed a miracle by feeding over five thousand (Luke 9:10-17).

Jesus sends all His disciples (including us) on a mission to represent Him to the world and to practice what we have learned from watching Him. He also reminds us that *He will always be with us*, even as we go with our human limitations (Matthew 28:18-20).

From Grace to Grace:

Throughout life, you are faced with opportunities to demonstrate that you have *mastered*, or are progressing in mastery of, an activity such as walking, writing your name, driving a car, or balancing a checkbook. In all stages of education, you are required to *test out* of various levels before advancing to the next level.

Because you have experienced the challenging process of mastery and know that growth takes time and comes through the courageous act of *testing out* and demonstrating how well the activity is understood or known, you can give others space and encouragement through their progression to mastery. *Grace* understands there will be setbacks or failures but continues to communicate support and belief in the person's ability to prevail and be successful.

I'm not afraid anymore.

On the Dance Floor:

Performing for the first time as a *spotlight* in front of the studio audience was terrifying because I was afraid of being watched, judged, compared with, dancing imperfectly, or not meeting someone else's expectations. However, the studio culture of *grace* encouraged solo performances to help students face and conquer fears of dancing in front of others.

During *spotlight* performances, I observed students of all age groups dancing at various skill levels. Each person—especially the Newcomer and Beginner—was cheered on. No special treatment or accolades were given to those with more experience. In fact, it seemed the more advanced students were the ones cheering the loudest because they remembered their starting point and their journey to overcoming the fear of performing in front of others.

I'm no longer afraid to dance in front of others or afraid of what people think. Though I still struggle with confidence in knowing steps and routines, I am no longer afraid to step on the dance floor. Over time, with experience and within the accepting culture of the studio, it is a relief to say that I am no longer afraid of what people will think. I dance for me, and I *dance for Jesus*.

Dancing with Jesus:

Jesus asked the blind man, *What do you want Me to do for you?* (Mark 10:51). I envisioned Jesus asking me the same question. My answer is that I want to conquer my fears and overcome my background of *people-pleasing*.

I want to dance freely (unafraid) and fully (to the best of my potential, as Jesus sees me).

I have been continually inviting Jesus into the broken places in my heart that have led to fear and asking Him to heal and restore me in those hurting places. The thief, Satan, wants to steal joy, but Jesus came for us to have *life to the full* (John 10:10). Living life in freedom! Freedom to dance! Freedom to dance fully and unafraid because I'm dancing on the dance floor of *Grace*.

Peace I leave with you; My peace I give you. I do not give to you as the world gives. Do not let your hearts be troubled and do not be afraid (John 14:27). Jesus desires that we live unafraid, trusting Him for all our needs.

From Grace to Grace:

As you grow in confidence that replaces fear, you can help others face their fears and help them feel safe and encouraged to keep pushing through their challenges. One Newcomer expressed her fears, so I asked, *Why are you afraid?* She thought about it and replied, *I'm afraid of failing.* Thankfully, I had the opportunity to share my *grace* journey in dance and told her, *You can't fail in dance. What's the worst-case scenario?* Worst case? You fall (which I have) and you pick yourself up and try again. There is nothing to be afraid of. We only fail when we paralyze ourselves by fear and stop dancing or living life.

Fear will keep us from becoming the best version of ourselves that God created. Facing fear is one of the biggest obstacles that we can help others overcome. Helping others to live fully and freely by trusting in Jesus is your greatest *grace* gift.

The man wears the number on his back.

On the Dance Floor:

This phrase is probably not obvious in its purpose and analogy, but after some thought, the concept was intriguing. A woman is associated with the man's competition number that he wears on his back. A woman competitor does not have her own identifying number because the number cannot be attached to her dress.

Remember that the purpose of the man is to present the woman as a beautiful picture. Most likely, a woman's dress will be bejeweled, with a low-cut style in the back, and made with delicate fabric. An attached number would be damaging and distracting.

Dancing with Jesus:

We are known by our association with Jesus—by the blood of Jesus. *In Him we have redemption through His blood, the forgiveness of sins, in accordance with the riches of God's grace* (Ephesians 1:7).

Our identity is *in Jesus*. We are *in Him*, associated *with Him* by wearing *His number,* which is *His blood.* We accepted the invitation to dance with Him and are known to the Father because of *HIM.*

Therefore, since we have a great high priest who has ascended into heaven, Jesus the Son of God, let us hold firmly to the faith we profess. For we do not have a high priest who is unable to empathize with our weaknesses, but we have one who has been tempted in every way, just as we are—yet He did not sin. Let us then approach God's throne of grace with confidence, so that we may receive mercy and find grace to help us in our time of need (Hebrews 4:14-16).

From Grace to Grace:

Because Jesus loves you, you love others. Because you are known by Jesus, you help bear the burdens of others and encourage them on their journey. There are times when you will willingly sacrifice to meet their needs—as your Jesus did—because of the overflow of your love and *grace*.

Are you inspired to sacrifice your needs for those who might need encouragement and support? Who needs to be introduced to the Love and *Grace* of Jesus?

Keep your eyes on me.

On the Dance Floor:

During competition the floor is crowded with numerous couples. When the music begins, it can seem chaotic with the variety of movements that take place in a small space. In preparation for one event, my partner John told me the most important thing to remember: *Keep your eyes on me. It's as if it is just the two of us on the dance floor.*

Our main goal on the floor was to dance connected as a unit—not to be concerned about what others thought of us or how they were dancing, but to dance as one, as if we were the only two people on the floor.

Dancing with Jesus:

Remember the story of the disciple Peter walking toward Jesus on the sea (Matthew 14:22-33)? He was fine until he took his eyes off Jesus and felt the wind swirling and saw the waves. He was afraid and started to sink.

Therefore, since we are surrounded by such a great cloud of witnesses, let us throw off everything that hinders and the sin that so easily entangles. And let us run with perseverance the race marked out for us, fixing our eyes on Jesus, the pioneer and perfecter of faith. For the joy set before Him He endured the cross, scorning its shame, and sat down at the right hand of the throne of God. Consider Him who endured such opposition from sinners, so that you will not grow weary and lose heart (Hebrews 12:1-3).

I'm inspired by the example of Mary Magdalene. She followed Him as one of His disciples during His ministry and refused to take her eyes off Him and leave His presence—even while He suffered on the cross and was quickly buried in a tomb. It is no wonder to me that Jesus first appeared to a woman who refused to take her eyes off Him and leave Him—even when she thought He was gone.

Who is it you are looking for? Jesus asked. *Mary!* He honored her dedication to Him by revealing Himself to her as the first witness of His resurrection (John 20:1-18).

From Grace to Grace:

Encourage others to keep their eyes on Jesus. Only Jesus sees, knows and is always present for comfort. He is the only One who saves, redeems, rescues and has strength to revive, restore and guide. And He honors those who continue their pursuit of His presence.

SILVER LEVEL

When I was invited to participate in the Silver-level group lessons, I was so excited because I felt that after a couple of foundational years, I had finally arrived! As a Newcomer and Bronze-level student, I would admire those students who were at the Silver-level and higher. Intuitively, I said to myself that when I could begin learning the Silver-level Viennese Waltz, I could say that I truly was a dancer.

Silver-level of dance adds more layers of technique to the foundations. Hip action, closed-body contact, performance techniques, and full-body dancing are introduced and emphasized. Patterns were more complex, and choreographed routines with *tricks* were introduced. I began dancing more independently (but still with a partner) and consistently entered more competitions.

At the Silver level, I noticed that I was developing my own individual style. Though I was stretching and growing in foundational technique, routines were choreographed to complement my physical ability and personality. Though I understood that my dance journey would be a lifelong journey, at the Silver level, I felt I had finally arrived and could confidently tell others that *I was a ballroom dancer*!

Layers are built upon a solid foundation.

On the Dance Floor:

New actions are added to the basic movement as the student develops. Layers of dance and performance techniques are added to foundations as the student is capable. It is a continually growing process, with nuances of technique enhancing a student's dance ability and performance.

Because I chose to learn to dance and found a safe place to grow, I trusted the stretching and growing process my instructors used to develop my dance abilities.

In contrast to the usual visual of a foundation laid at the bottom of a structure, during this phase of dance, the foundational frame (the *upstairs*) must be set in stone and solid. Then the *downstairs* aspects of dance (steps, hip action) will follow.

Dancing with Jesus:

Jesus grew in wisdom, stature and favor with God and man (Luke 2:52). He grew from a child into adulthood with *layers* added to His foundation as he was physically, mentally, emotionally and spiritually capable.

Though the process of growth is sometimes hard and difficult, I trust the Master as He gently guides me to higher levels. Through the process of building my relationship with Jesus, He reminds me that *His yoke is easy, and His burden is light* (Matthew 11:30).

I am also reminded to establish and build my foundation carefully. *For no one can lay any foundation other than the one already laid, which is Jesus Christ. If anyone builds on this foundation using gold, silver, costly stones, wood, hay or straw, their work will be shown for what it is, because the Day will bring it to light. It will be revealed with fire, and the fire will test the quality of each person's work. If what has been built survives, the builder will receive a reward. If it is burned up, the builder will suffer loss but yet will be saved—even though only as one escaping through the flames* (1 Corinthians 3:11-15).

From Grace to Grace:

Growth is a process, and *grace* provides a safe environment in which to grow. You can facilitate the growth of others by patiently giving them *grace and space* to lay down and build upon strong foundations. You remind them not to rush the process or take shortcuts because they will benefit in the long run. Mastery of any subject, talent, or skill takes time.

Discouragement can set in during the early stages of development because it might be challenging to see any progress, especially when quick results are desired. But your gift of encouragement is of immeasurable value if you can help others see that being patient with the process of laying upon a strong and lasting foundation will reap huge rewards.

Increased connection

On the Dance Floor:

As the dance partnership and relationship grows, connection is increased by closer body contact. There is less space within the frame as the connection of ribs and hips allows for more synchronous movement.

Just as in the beginning levels, the increase in body connection is unforced by the man but develops naturally as the woman trusts the Leader. The closer body contact allows the dance couple to dance more fully as one.

Dancing with Jesus:

Our relationship with Jesus grows as we stay attached to Him.

Abide in Me, and I in you. As the branch cannot bear fruit of itself, unless it abides in the vine, neither can you, unless you abide in Me. I am the vine, you are the branches. He who abides in Me, and I in him, bears much fruit; for without Me you can do nothing (John 15:4-5).

As we stay attached and connected to Jesus, the Vine, we dance more closely as one.

I do not pray for these alone, but also for those who will believe in Me through their word; that they all may be one, as You, Father, are in Me, and I in You; that they also may be one in Us, that the world may believe that You sent Me. And the glory which You gave Me I have given them, that they may be one just as We are one: I in them, and You in Me; that they may be made perfect in one, and that the world may know that You have sent Me and have loved them as You have loved Me (John 17:20-23).

From Grace to Grace:

Developing a relationship takes mutual desire and intentional investment of time. As two individuals grow closer, each individual stays connected in a variety of ways. The progression begins with head knowledge of each other, then stronger heart connection into oneness.

One of the themes of this book is the importance of dancing within a relationship of human and divine connection. Are you more watchful for individuals who seem to be isolated, lonely or disconnected from social groups? I pray that you will have a new perspective that can see individuals who need to be invited into a community.

That's the best you've ever done.

On the Dance Floor:

I'm proud of you! That's the best you've ever done, but don't be surprised if you don't do it as well next time. At least you know that it is going into your muscle memory, and it will get more consistently better with practice.

Just as with any quest to acquire a new skill, it seems there is more frustration with lack of progress than acknowledgment of progress. For every compliment given, there have been numerous hours of repetition, critique, practice, setbacks, and discouragement.

Therefore, when an affirmation of mastery is given, not only is it rare, but in my case, it is cherished and becomes the fuel to keep me moving forward toward my goal of dancing beautifully.

I was happy to hear that my coach was pleased with my performance and felt a sense of relief to know that there was no expectation of perfection. *Grace* would be extended to me as I gained consistency in a new skill.

Dancing with Jesus:

Well done, good and faithful servant . . . you have been faithful with a little . . . (Matthew 25:14-30). God gives us talents and expects them to be used and grown. It pleases Him when we honor Him with our courageous and consistent growth.

I love the example of Jesus' friend, Mary of Bethany. She honored Jesus publicly with her treasure and it pleased Jesus. He *graciously* commended her by stating, *She did what she could. She has done a beautiful thing for Me* (Matthew 26:6-13, Mark 14:1-9).

Jesus sent disciples to heal and cast out demons, but on one occasion they seem to have *failed* in their mission and asked Jesus why. Jesus didn't call out their failure or shame them but told them there was more to be learned (Mark 9:14-29).

Jesus expects that we continue to learn and grow, but thankfully, He is patient with us during our challenging and unending journey to reflect Him.

From Grace to Grace:

Because you know how an encouraging word can fuel your enthusiasm to continue to persevere through a challenge, you can offer genuine affirmations to others. *Grace* senses when an individual needs to be reminded of the reason they chose a growth journey when they might not see the results they hoped for.

A well-timed compliment and acknowledgment that their hard work is seen can be the fuel for a friend or family member to continue when their spirits are flagging or when they want to give up. You can remind them that they eventually *will* reap the benefits they are seeking if they continue on the growth path.

I see you as my partner.

On the Dance Floor:

Yes, technically you are my student, but I see you now as my partner. This statement impacted me tremendously because it implied a mutual relationship. My professional partner retained his status as the Pro, but now I, as an Amateur, shared equal responsibility when competing as a team.

My goal shifted from relying on my Pro as the primary person in the partnership to the realization that I, too, had a role in contributing to the performance of our team so that my Pro was also enjoying the dance at a higher level.

Dancing with Jesus:

No longer do I call you servants, for a servant does not know what his master is doing; but I have called you friends, for all things that I heard from My Father I have made known to you (John 15:15).

My relationship with Jesus has changed as I have danced with Him through the years. At first, His role as Savior, Rescuer, Inviter, Pursuer, and Lord affected how I danced with Him—carefully and at a bit of a distance. But, as I have experienced more of who He is in my life, I have *layered* onto the foundation of Savior and Lord, the intimate relationship of Friend. He leads, and I follow, but with the confidence that He has invited me into the unity of sharing Love from and with the Father and Spirit.

From Grace to Grace:

Throughout your life, you play a variety of relational roles: employer/employee, mentor/mentee, husband/wife, parent/child. Many times, these roles begin with a *hierarchy*, but over time, the relationship will grow into a more equal relationship of two individuals who are working together as partners and peers toward a shared goal.

Just as in the relationship with Jesus, the rare few who we share heart-to-heart journeys and consider as friends are the most special and impact us greatly through life. Can you identify a few of the most cherished individuals in your life who you count as peers, partners, and true friends?

Use your partner's strength.

On the Dance Floor:

As a dancer progresses from solely relying on her partner to lead, she dances more independently. But there comes a point in her training where *tricks* and choreography become more complex. Some poses require the partner to help hold the position so that he can shape her into one that she couldn't do on her own. *Your partner is there to rely on, so use his strength. Use the hold to your advantage. Rely on his strength; trust him to hold you.*

At times, the dance journey seems contradictory. As the student progresses, she or he is encouraged to dance independently. AND the message is also to be dependent and use the partner's strength. Be independent AND dependent.

Dancing with Jesus:

As we progress in our spiritual growth from a new follower of Jesus to being sent out and entrusted and empowered with gifts of the Spirit, we are reminded to continue to stay attached to Him.

Without Me you can do nothing (John 15:5).

With God, nothing is impossible (Matthew 19:26; Mark 10:27).

Your right hand has held me up; Your help has made me great (Psalm 18:35).

We are both independent (sent out on mission and ministry) AND dependent on Jesus for His strength and guidance. It does make for an interesting dance.

From Grace to Grace:

The most successful relationships are those that are established on independence AND dependence. We need to be reminded that though we can *hold our own frame up*, we can achieve even greater things when working in partnerships and teams and by using the strengths of the community to support and facilitate growth.

You dance too safe.

On the Dance Floor:

Though this phrase had the most impact when spoken by Charisma, the first person I met when I started my ballroom dance journey in the Arthur Murray Costa Mesa studio, it seemed to be a common theme that my instructors had been implying since the beginning of my journey. Though I've grown in many areas and aspects of dance, Charisma pinpointed that dancing *too safe* continues to be my biggest challenge.

To express oneself freely and fully, a dancer must take risks and step out of their comfort zones. What am I afraid of? Why do I revert to *safe*? My instructor John described it as if I'm wearing a white dress that I've taken great care of and go to great lengths to make sure that it stays pure and white—safe and cautious. John used the phrase, *get messy,* encouraging me to take risks, break my beautiful dance lines and throw myself into the dance moves emotionally and physically.

Dancing with Jesus:

The analogy of being careful to protect my white dress was quite insightful. From my childhood I was careful about my behavior because I have a reverence for God's Law. I wanted to please God and be a *good girl*. I was careful and thoughtful of the choices I made. The motive was right, but over time I became performance-oriented and focused about *doing the right thing*. The heart relationship with Jesus was lost in the process. Thankfully, God opened my eyes to that flawed theology and has been *undoing* my tendency to be a *safe and careful doer*.

Now, I dance with Jesus in a white dress (or one with many colors) and am still careful not to cause damage to my dress out of love and respect. My desire is to present a beautifully free heart as I *dance with Jesus*. Through God's Spirit, I am empowered to go beyond my *natural self* with Christ living in me and making me boldly confident.

In the parable of talents, the phrase *I was afraid, so I hid* (Matthew 25:24-25) jumped out at me and solidified my commitment to overcome timidity in all areas of my life. I reminded myself that Jesus would be more than pleased to assist me to conquer fears and to not dance or live *too safe*. Truly, *I can do all things through Christ who gives me strength* (Philippians 4:13). I could have self-control (a fruit of the Spirit) AND surrender my control to Jesus. Like Peter, I could step out of the safety of the boat and walk on water IF I kept my eyes on Jesus.

Jesus got *messy*. He wasn't afraid to touch an unclean person such as the leper. He spoke with people who were outside his *safe*, pure-white *safe* zone. He ate with people with less than glowing reputations, such as tax collectors. The ultimate act of not being *safe* was demonstrated by Jesus on the cross. Angels could have rescued Him. Instead, He allowed Himself to be scourged beyond recognition and nailed to a cross covered with His blood, sweat and tears so that all humanity would be forgiven and be able to wear pure white robes of His righteousness for all eternity (Isaiah 61:10; Revelation 7:13-15).

From Grace to Grace:

When you give up any pretensions of perfection and allow the authentic self to love as Jesus loved, you want to share His *Grace* with everyone you encounter, even if they seem to be outside your sanitized sphere. You want to befriend those who others shun, such as the homeless, marginalized or societal outcasts. You love all people with the same love that Jesus demonstrated. He died for ALL, so you love ALL. You allow yourself to step out of the performance mode of *safe* and into heartfelt *messy* to share His Love and *Grace*.

Where is God calling you out of your comfort in order to grow, but you are too afraid? Is it time to surrender and trust His lead?

The man's role is to make the woman feel safe.

On the Dance Floor:

The man's role is to make the woman feel safe. Why? *SO THAT she can be beautiful.* This phrase was spoken by Matt on the same day Charisma said that I danced *too safe*.

Safe can have two contextual meanings. On the one hand, I want to stretch and abandon control so that I can dance more fully and uninhibitedly. On the other hand, within this context, it is important to establish an atmosphere and environment *so that* a woman can feel *safe* to let go, surrendering control and inhibitions. When she feels *safe—safe* to explore, *safe* not to be judged or compared, *safe* to grow—she dances fully and freely (*not safe*).

A *safe* partnership is one of *grace*. In an atmosphere of *grace* I was encouraged emotionally. I felt *safe* to be beautiful and reach my potential. I felt *safe* to fail and to push past emotionally and physically perceived boundaries. Within this *safe* environment and partnership, I felt free to thrive and dance more beautifully.

Dancing with Jesus:

There were many times Jesus defended a woman, thereby making her feel *safe* (Mark 14:1-9). Jesus healed, restored, listened to, and comforted women. His loving and *gracious* interaction with a woman spoke to her heart and made her feel *safe* with Him. He showed that she had value and that she could trust Him.

Jesus' nature was one of *Grace* and acceptance. Even in the midst of an unaccepting culture, His presence, along with His words and deeds, created a *safe* environment for a woman to be fully free to be in a relationship with Him (Luke 7:36-50, 10:38-42; John 4:1-42).

From Grace to Grace:

I hope that my legacy as a mommy will be one where my children thrived and grew up to their potential because they lived in a household of *grace* where they felt *safe* to learn because they received encouragement and patience. I hope they felt *safe* to take risks, to stretch, to push emotional and physical boundaries on their path because they knew their mom believed in their God-given potential.

An individual feels *safe* physically when he or she is protected and provided for. Feeling *safe* emotionally comes from a culture of unconditional love where a person is delighted in. Influential others are attentive to his or her needs, not displeased or distant. A child trusts the parent will come to his or her defense and won't abandon him or her.

When you understand the importance that a *safe* environment (*grace*) has on your growth, it becomes important for you to create a *safe* environment so that your family and friends can grow.

Sacrifice is required.

On the Dance Floor:

Matt explained that as the partnership grows and dance moves become more complex—even riskier—the man's role continues to primarily facilitate the woman's role of looking beautiful. The man's role is to help the woman look good—even if it means he sacrifices his position. As she takes greater risks with moves and poses, the man must use his strength and position to keep her stable and supported—even if it means that he might be moved out of position or not look as good himself.

Because the man is navigating the woman around the floor at greater speeds and with more complex movements, his role is to be increasingly watchful and navigate around obstacles (usually other dance partners moving at equally fast speeds) so that she is able to fully express herself and to showcase the movements.

Part of the giggle of the Matt-Barb partnership was that sometimes I would not read his signals correctly, would incorrectly anticipate his next move, or would forget what came next. *What moves are we going to make up today?* he teasingly would ask.

But Matt would also tell me that whatever I would make up, or however I would dance, it was his role to adjust and to make me look good. *You don't have to fix it—I will.* There was comfort in knowing that his role was to fix my missteps. Obviously, I would try to do my best, but his primary role was to help me look beautiful.

Dancing with Jesus:

Greater love has no one than this: to lay down one's life for his friends (John 15:13). Jesus sacrificed Himself for each one of us, specifically for our ultimate *success*—eternity with Him. He sacrificed His position of divinity, came to earth, became a servant, lived among us, and paid the penalty for something we could not do by ourselves. He literally sacrificed His position of divinity and willingly took on the position of the cross (Philippians 2:6-8).

His sacrifice on our behalf was due to His *Grace*, not because of any goodness or good deeds of our own (Ephesians 2:4-10).

Jesus came to serve, not to be served (Matthew 20:28). And His greatest act of service to us individually and to the world was His sacrifice on the cross for our sins.

From Grace to Grace:

As parents, with our gift of love, we sacrifice in many ways—even diminishing our position and needs so that our children can grow into their potential.

When you have received *grace*, you are more willing to *sacrifice* your time, position, money or in numerous other ways to help others be successful. *Grace* extended to you encourages you to follow Jesus' example by loving others and laying down your life to serve them.

I've got you. I won't allow you to fall.

On the Dance Floor:

As I progressed in ability and complexity of routines, there were times when John stretched me to the point I would be unable to hold myself while extended on one foot. I had to trust in the pro's ability to support me during those moments when I was no longer on my own balance.

Multiple times, I would hear my partner say, *I've got you.* The implicit message was, *I won't walk away. I'm invested in protecting you. I'm committed to you and to your success.*

Dancing with Jesus:

When dancing with Jesus, there are many times when He asks us to go where we are uncomfortable and stretches us in ways that seem to take us off balance. *The Lord makes firm the steps of the one who delights in Him; though he may stumble, he will not fall, for the Lord upholds him with His hand* (Psalm 37:23-24).

Jesus also reminds me that while I'm dancing with Him, *He won't ever leave or forsake me; He will be with me always* (Hebrews 13:5).

Thankfully, I am secure in my future—the ultimate security—because of Jesus.

I give them eternal life and they will never perish; no one will snatch them out of my hand. My Father, who has given them to Me, is greater than all; and no one is able to snatch them out of My Father's hand (John 10:28-29).

From Grace to Grace:

This analogy works within a relationship (on the dance floor, with Jesus, and with others) when partners are actively dancing with each other. The assumption is that there isn't rebellion and willingly walking away from the relationship.

Sometimes as parents, we allow our children safe space to stumble or fall and to reap the consequences of poor choices. We choose not to rescue them when we know the learning experience of *falling* benefits their growth.

When parenting with *grace*, you never let go of supporting them in their growth journey. You believe in their ability to stretch and grow—and to even face *failure*—but *grace* always says, *I love you unconditionally, even to the point I'll never stop holding on even when challenges seem impossible or overwhelming.*

Keep moving in the direction the Lead initiates.

On the Dance Floor:

One of the foundational lessons in dance relates to *direction*. A woman continues in the direction established by the man until he initiates a change in direction. This change in direction is best communicated through my consistent connection with my partner.

I trust that my partner, the Leader, sees the perspective of the entire floor and knows the pattern more clearly than I do. I trust he sees the bigger picture because that is his role. He knows what patterns to include for the overall success of our dancing unit and to make me look beautiful.

When I lose connection with my Leader, we lose momentum and dance out of sync because I guess or anticipate where I think we are headed. Yes, my Leader can fix my missteps, but the better way is to stay connected, trust him completely, and follow his lead.

Dancing with Jesus:

When I trust in Jesus' plans for my life, I continue to go in the direction He established until He changes the growth trajectory.

We can trust that Jesus sees the bigger eternal picture and knows where He wants us to go next. Can Jesus *fix* or redeem our detours when we go off on our own? Of course, but the preferred way (without negative consequences) is to first trust and follow our Leader, Jesus.

Sometimes, we don't clearly hear the next step to take, so we give up waiting and take matters into our own hands. Remember the story of Abraham and Sarah? The promise that God made to them didn't happen in *their* time frame, so they took a detour that caused generational challenges (Genesis 15, 16, 17, 18, 21). God *fixed* and redeemed their story, but the negative generational consequences of not believing and waiting for the directional change of God caused difficulties and repercussions that could have been prevented.

From Grace to Grace:

Trust and patience are required to keep moving forward until it becomes clear to change direction. Though challenging, you can learn to listen expectantly to the Leader—both on the dance floor and with Jesus—and trust that He will initiate and communicate the next direction to take based on His eternal perspective and master plan for your life.

I'm getting better every day!

On the Dance Floor:

Regardless of setbacks, I keep moving forward. Yes, I'm not where I want to be, but I refuse to compare my journey with the journey of another or allow myself to get discouraged with where I am or what level I'm dancing at. I remind myself that every time I choose to step onto the dance floor with an open mind and face the anxiety and reality that *this-is-not-easy*, I improve.

It is a gift to be able to take dance lessons, so I choose to keep a positive outlook and be grateful each time I step through the studio doors. I have to remind myself to *be patient and give myself grace.*

Dancing with Jesus:

Not that I have already obtained all this or have already arrived at my goal, but I press on to take hold of that for which Christ Jesus took hold of me. Brothers and sisters, I do not consider myself yet to have taken hold of it. But one thing I do: Forgetting what is behind and straining toward, reaching forward to what is ahead, I press on toward the goal to win the prize for which God has called me heavenward in Christ Jesus (Philippians 3:12-14).

The *dance with Jesus* is an intentional one of choice and forward movement, pressing toward the goal and prize of eternity.

From Grace to Grace:

As a lifelong learner, choose to continue to learn something new such as a language or a new activity. You may never become a professional, but you certainly will be a better dancer, artist, musician (or whatever) if you just start making consistent progress toward your goals every day.

One of my personal mottos is *onwards and upwards.* I remind myself to keep moving forward—growing every day in an area of life. Don't be content to sit on the sidelines and watch. Choose to consistently be a participant, and over a period of time, you will see that you are getting better and gaining expertise every day.

Growing in strength

On the Dance Floor:

While initiating a turn, a visiting coach spun me out so forcefully that I lost my balance and fell—*gracefully*, of course. My skill level and body control could not manage his strength, and because he was not my regular instructor, he wasn't aware of my current abilities.

At times I've had to let my instructor know there were certain actions that I was not yet capable of performing. My skill level, age, or previous injury brought physical limitations.

By working within those limitations, not only did I grow in strength, but I could also overcome previous challenges and setbacks. The mindset is to continue to move forward and be determined to grow.

Dancing with Jesus:

Thankfully, God knows every aspect of our journey of growth and what is best for us (Psalm 139). There were times when Jesus was abrupt and communicated directly with those He encountered. And there were times when Jesus interacted with the qualities of a gentleman, not heavy-handed. He knew exactly how to interact with each individual so as to facilitate his or her journey.

For those who are emotionally broken, He treated them tenderly (Matthew 12:20). For those who are beleaguered, His requirements are easy, and the burden is light (Matthew 11:30).

Remember that our *Heavenly Father even knows what we need before we ask* (Matthew 6:8). We can trust that the Father knows how to maximize our growth, even if that includes correction (John 15:1-2).

Regardless of obstacles and challenges, *be on your guard; stand firm in the faith; be courageous; be strong* (1 Corinthians 16:13). The result is increased strength and capacity toward mastery.

From Grace to Grace:

    Learn to see others through Jesus' eyes. Be sensitive and graceful toward people you interact with. Try to understand their frame and where they are in their journey and react accordingly. They may be fragile emotionally and need tenderness and compassion. You become a true friend when you help them grow stronger by courageously facing their challenges.

Go out and shine.

On the Dance Floor:

Before our first competition as a new partnership, my coach, Kurt, encouraged me by saying, *You've got this, Barb. Go out and shine.* His reassuring words, *I've got you,* and *You can do this,* provided emotional support so that I felt safe to go onto the floor and shine! The pro's role is to encourage the participant, even in her insecurity. I danced safely and beautifully when I knew the goal of the pro was to assist me in dancing freely and fully.

Another way to *go out and shine* on the dance floor is by wearing colorful and shimmery dresses that reflect light. With emotional encouragement and confidence in my overall beautiful appearance, I could *go out and shine.*

Dancing with Jesus:

Jesus said that He is the *light of the world* (John 9:5). *In the beginning was the Word, and the Word was with God, and the Word was God. He was with God in the beginning. Through Him all things were made; without Him nothing was made that has been made. In Him was life, and that life was the light of all mankind. The light shines in the darkness, and the darkness has not overcome it* (John 1:1-5).

As we reflect Jesus, we are the *light of the world* (Matthew 5:14). Go out and shine! *Neither do people light a lamp and put it under a bowl. Instead, they put it on its stand, and it gives light to everyone in the house. In the same way, let your light shine before others, that they may see your good deeds and glorify your Father in heaven* (Matthew 5:15-16).

As followers of Jesus, we are called *a chosen generation, a royal priesthood, a holy nation, His own special people, that you may proclaim the praises of Him who called you out of darkness into His marvelous light* (1 Peter 2:9).

From Grace to Grace:

A word of encouragement goes a long way when a person is unsure of the next steps or afraid of failure or not measuring up to an expectation. *Go out and shine. Be the best version of yourself. I believe in you and can't wait to see your shimmering self that has been unveiled.*

Grace believes the best in a person. *Grace* reminds a person that there are choices he or she can make that bring out the beautiful shine for others to see.

I need more from you.

On the Dance Floor:

Come on, breathe and pull yourself together. I need more energy from you. The filter in my head heard *You are not enough. You are not doing enough.* Why is this phrase in a book about experiencing *grace* on the dance floor? It is to demonstrate the contrast to *grace*, which is a performance-orientation. Sadly, this message came through during one of my competitions. Because of my attempt to grow out of a performance-mentality, his comments sent me into an emotional dive. Instead of inspiring me to step up my performance, it was extremely counterproductive.

When these words were spoken by my dance partner, it implied that what I was doing was not enough; I was not good enough; I was not trying hard enough. Because of my sub-par performance (in the eyes of my partner), he walked away and distanced himself from me. I did not feel safe to dance freely because I was affected by the message that my partner was disappointed in me. I was not meeting his expectations.

Many have a view of God who is primarily concerned with performance. And when we view ourselves as *less*, for whatever reason, our filter says that God is so disappointed that He turns His back and walks away. Thankfully, the phrase I heard from my partner and that I interpreted as not being good enough and a disappointment was a one-time occurrence. It made such a contrasting impression on me that I knew that it must be included in the book.

Performance-orientation implies an emphasis on *doing* and earning approval versus *grace*-orientation, which emphasizes unconditional belief in who a person is and is becoming. It is the difference between the head and heart.

Dancing with Jesus:

The starting point of *dancing with Jesus* is *Grace*. *By grace you are saved . . . it is the gift of God . . . not by works* (Ephesians 2:8-10). Works are part of the equation, but not the starting point.

For God did not send His Son into the world to condemn the world, but that the world through Him might be saved (John 3:17).

The thief only comes to steal, and to kill, and to destroy. I have come that they may have life, and that they may have it more abundantly (John 10:10). The thief takes away joy through condemnation.

Jesus saves! He doesn't condemn. He doesn't require jumping through hoops or having to take specific steps or doing it perfectly for Him to love us and dance with us. Within that *Grace*-filled relationship built on *Grace* and Love, we thrive and grow, producing good works.

From Grace to Grace:

You give *grace* to others when you acknowledge that he or she is dancing beautifully where they are. The goal is to encourage through *grace*—which motivates a person—in contrast to implying the person is *less than* or *not good enough* or *a disappointment*.

Grace doesn't judge heart motives or condemn. *Grace* inspires others to grow within an environment of patience and belief in who they person is striving to become.

Grace also doesn't enable or condone behavior that is harmful, but it does encourage growth because of the foundational culture that includes patience and forgiveness while on the path toward becoming the best version that God created.

A collision of journeys

On the Dance Floor:

Because of the close proximity of dancing couples, it is not uncommon for physical contact to be made. There are occasional collisions, typically minor, when a foot gets stepped on. But especially at the higher levels of competition, where couples are traveling around the floor at high levels of speed, collisions can knock a person to the floor. While observing a pro-competition, two couples collided, and one of the male pros hit the floor and landed on his back. Thankfully, no one was injured, and he got up and continued through their routine.

There are also collisions of the *emotional* kind. That is when two dancers with unique journeys are challenged in such a way that feelings get hurt. As I previously described, the tone with which my pro partner addressed a challenging situation on the dance floor was filtered through my performance-oriented (non-*grace*) experience, and I reacted emotionally, thinking he was disappointed in me. Essentially, our two unique journeys collided, and a new opportunity presented itself to grow from the situation.

Dancing with Jesus:

Because Jesus came to the earth as the Son of God and Son of Man, whenever a human *collided* and encountered the divinity of Jesus, the person's journey and life trajectory were changed. The impact was profound.

Within the context of a collision with Jesus, a widow was burying her only son when she *collided* with Jesus. He saw her from a distance, had compassion on her and raised her son back to life (Luke 7:11-17).

A lonely Samaritan woman *collided* with Jesus in the heat of the day while drawing water from the well. During the conversation (shockingly, He was actually talking to a woman—a Samaritan woman) He revealed Himself as the Messiah (John 4:1-42).

While hanging on the cross, falsely accused, Jesus *collided* with a justly accused criminal who acknowledged Jesus as Lord (Luke 23:32-43).

Collisions with Jesus showcased His Love and *Grace*.

From Grace to Grace:

When we, as broken and incomplete humans, figuratively collide with each other, sometimes we get stepped on, knocked down, or injured. It takes *grace* to forgive and restore relationships. *Grace* gives the other person the benefit of the doubt and continues to believe in the person and love unconditionally. I remind myself that each individual is on his or her own growth path and that I am not responsible for his or her journey.

Because you are given *Grace* from Jesus, you can impact others with *grace*, peace, and restoration.

I could never be mad at you.

On the Dance Floor:

A performance-based culture says, *I'm only pleased with you when you perform as I expected.* In other words, the message is that either *You're not enough* or *You're too much*. When I sense disapproval from someone, my filter hears *I'm disappointed with you and I am distancing myself from you until you earn back my good graces.*

During the competition, when my pro partner indicated by words and actions that I didn't live up to his expectations, I felt deflated. In contrast, when one of the other pros read my emotional reaction and inquired about the situation, he responded with the reassuring words, *Barb, I could never be mad at you.*

Dancing with Jesus:

Jesus never gave up on His disciple Peter, even after several episodes of *disappointment* with his behavior. On one occasion, Peter confronted Jesus and in turn, Jesus rebuked him (Matthew 16:21-23; Mark 8:31-33). Even after Peter presumptuously cut off a man's ear during Jesus' arrest (John 18:9-11) and after he denied Jesus three times before His crucifixion (Luke 22:31-34, 54-62), Jesus didn't give up on him. He *graciously* restored their relationship after His resurrection (John 21:1-19).

When Jesus' friend Martha exploded in frustration because of her sister Mary's lack of involvement with the chores, Jesus calmly settled her down. He maintained a posture of *Grace* toward her while giving her a more complete perspective of life (Luke 10:38-42).

Jesus commands us to *be perfect* (Matthew 5:48), but He doesn't abandon us when we inevitably fall short of perfection while in the process of growth.

Thankfully, Jesus is on our side and is *for* us, even though we don't deserve His *Grace*. *Who then is the one who condemns? No one. Christ Jesus who died—more than that, who was raised to life—is at the right hand of God and is also interceding for us* (Romans 8:34).

From Grace to Grace:

Give others *grace*. Don't judge them—you don't know their story, motives, or where they are on their journey. If they are *dancing with Jesus*, He has them in His grasp, and you can trust and believe that Jesus knows the path they are on.

Yes, we humans fail each other and hurt each other's feelings. But *grace* believes in the other person's journey and encourages him or her to keep moving forward toward perfection.

Grace does not distance your heart from a person—even when you are hurt by them. *Grace* forgives and believes the best—even when you are humanly disappointed. *Grace* loves a person for whom he or she is—not for what a person says, or does, or for how their behavior impacts you, each person is on an individual journey with Jesus. Give them *grace*.

I won't let you give up on yourself.

On the Dance Floor:

During the competition where I had a *collision of journeys* with my instructor and filtered his response through my performance mentality, I was discouraged and ready to quit competing. I considered walking away from the most challenging aspects of my dance experience—choreographed routines. Another studio amateur, Susan, told me, *Regardless of what happened, I won't let you give up on yourself!*

It would have been a rash, emotional decision at the moment to give up on an aspect of my dance journey that was challenging. Susan reminded me that everyone in the dance community—even the pros—has faced disappointments and setbacks and felt like giving up. But she encouraged me that this situation would resolve and that I would continue to grow if I didn't give up.

Dancing with Jesus:

After denying Jesus three times during his trial, Peter was convicted of this grievous offense and wanted to quit (Matthew 29:69-76; Luke 22:62). After the death of his master, Peter went back to fishing, not knowing what else to do. But Jesus wanted to restore Peter. When an angel told the disciples where to meet Jesus after His resurrection, he specifically mentioned Peter by name (Mark 16:7), because Jesus was inviting him back into a relationship.

Jesus intentionally spent time with Peter and with uncommon *Grace* and unconditional Love restored their relationship (John 21:1-19). Jesus essentially said to Peter, *I won't let you give up on yourself.* When He commissioned him to share the Good News of Jesus and empowered him with the Holy Spirit, the world has not been the same.

From Grace to Grace:

When you see what a person is capable of (*though they may not believe it themselves*) or what potential they have (*though they may not see it themselves*), you intentionally become their advocate of *grace* and speak words of truth into their lives. You can encourage them not to quit the journey when facing challenges, obstacles, or setbacks.

What person comes to mind who might need a word of encouragement? Are you able to recognize the body language of someone who is struggling emotionally or overwhelmed? How would a word of *grace* change their perspective and brighten their day?

I've been there.

On the Dance Floor:

I've been in your shoes. The pros were not the only ones who supported me. The studio amateur students also provided encouragement. They walked and danced a similar—though unique—journey several years before me. They understood the challenges, the changes a person would go through, the adjustments one must make for injuries, adapting to new coaches, dealing with disappointments, handling stress and expectations of competitions.

As I grew into higher levels of dance and was exposed to new aspects of the dance journey, it was helpful to solicit advice from my fellow students who had more experience than I did. And in turn, I was able to offer encouragement to the newer students who were advancing into aspects that I felt comfortable with.

Dancing with Jesus:

I'm grateful that we have the Bible, which is documentation of individuals who have walked through life and faced similar challenges. The stories of faithful women and men inspire me and give me hope when I am struggling in the midst of a storm.

Therefore, since we are surrounded by so great a cloud of witnesses, let us lay aside every weight, and the sin which so easily ensnares us, and let us run with endurance the race that is set before us . . . (Hebrews 12:1).

And we have the stories of our faithful Jesus. *It's obvious, of course, that he didn't go to all this trouble for angels. It was for people like us, children of Abraham. That's why he had to enter into every detail of human life. Then, when he came before God as high priest to get rid of the people's sins, he would have already experienced it all himself—all the pain, all the testing—and would be able to help where help was needed* (Hebrews 2:16-18 The Message).

Jesus suffered and experienced weakness (Hebrews 5:1-10) and can help us when we are tempted and tested (Hebrews 2:18). Therefore, when we are in need, *we can approach God's throne of grace with confidence and boldness, so that we may receive mercy and find grace to help us in our time of need* (Hebrews 4:16).

From Grace to Grace:

Because you have walked through life's challenges, you can bolster the courage of someone who is facing a setback or hardship. Those who have suffered through a health trial tend to have a special empathy for those walking a similar path. You can use your challenges and subsequent victories to encourage those who are in the midst of a trying time. *I've been there, I understand. Hang in there!*

Your greatest gift to another person in their time of need is to share with them the love of Jesus and tell them that Jesus *has been there and is the only One who can provide the peace, mercy and Grace you are seeking.*

Do not be discouraged.

On the Dance Floor:

During my newer phases of growth (and especially during the *collision of journeys* incident), I became so discouraged that it affected the entire competition day and the following week of studio classes. Discouragement immobilized me, and I couldn't seem to shake it emotionally and regroup.

However, because I was determined to participate in a lifelong dance journey, I reminded myself that minor setbacks did not define who I was as a dancer or as a person.

As with any new learning opportunity, not every performance would be stellar. If I didn't have my best heat in one competition, I knew there would be others. In the overall scheme of life, what was the worst thing that could happen at a competition? I could fall in an ungraceful way (which I saw one of the pros do). If I didn't score well and missed an opportunity for a featured final round, who would really care in the long run? In time, disappointing moments would be forgotten if I did not allow myself to become discouraged.

Dancing with Jesus:

When *dancing with Jesus* as one of His believers and disciples, eternity is not at stake unless I walk away from the *dance with Jesus*, denying His invitation to join Him.

And I give them eternal life, and they shall never perish; neither shall anyone snatch them out of My hand. My Father, who has given them to Me, is greater than all; and no one is able to snatch them out of My Father's hand. My Father and I are one (John 10:28-30).

Jesus will be with me always and will never leave or forsake me (Matthew 28:20; Hebrews 13:5). *I am confident that God will be faithful to complete the work in me* as long as I continue to dance with Him (Philippians 1:6). I will have missteps through my journey, but I'm reminded not to become discouraged because Jesus is with me and working in me through His Spirit.

If I continue to move forward in my journey, *I will see progress and reap what has been sown, if I do not lose heart* (Galatians 6:9).

May our Lord Jesus Christ himself and God our Father, who loved us and by His grace gave us eternal encouragement and good hope, encourage your hearts and strengthen you in every good deed and word (2 Thessalonians 2:16-17).

From Grace to Grace:

There are seasons in life that seem to be particularly challenging and disappointing. As you navigate discouraging incidents or chapters, you will personally grow in your faith and hope for the bigger perspective if you keep your eyes on Jesus.

You can also speak into the lives of those who are weary and discouraged and who are sitting on the sidelines catching their breath or recuperating from a fall. You can be a voice of comfort and encouragement and find tangible ways to lift one's eyes up or help them to rest.

Though *comfort* is more commonly linked with sorrow or grief, I believe comfort given to others when they are discouraged is an antidote to their emotional state. *As we have been comforted by God, we can comfort others when they are suffering or facing troubles* (2 Corinthians 1:3-6).

I'm sorry. Please forgive me.

On the Dance Floor:

An atmosphere of *grace* in the studio created a safe environment where a mutual discussion to voice my *hurt* regarding the *collision of journeys* could take place. Thankfully, my instructor genuinely wanted to know how the comment *I need more from you* impacted me emotionally. I took ownership of my filter—that of performance-orientation and people-pleasing—not blaming my instructor. Yes, it hurt, but I felt safe to say, *You hurt me, and it affected me emotionally.*

He didn't get offended or blame me for the situation or reaction. He explained his journey—wanting the best for me—but said that was not an excuse for the demanding tone and walking away. My instructor took ownership of his motivation—wanting more from me—and genuinely said, *I'm sorry. I can see how that would have been perceived. I didn't mean to hurt you. Please forgive me.*

Because the atmosphere of *grace* facilitated forgiveness, reconciliation, and hugs followed.

Dancing with Jesus:

The analogy of the professional saying, *I'm sorry* breaks down at this point, because Jesus is *NOT* the one who says, *I'm sorry, please forgive Me.* Our human response when encountering the divine Jesus is for US to say, *I'm sorry, please forgive me.* And because of His Love and *Grace*, He does forgive and restore our broken relationship with our Heavenly Father (Colossians 1:13-14).

Only Jesus had the authority on earth to say, *Your sins are forgiven* (Matthew 9:6, Mark 2:10). Before His ordeal on the cross where He bore our sins, He stated that *His blood was poured out for the forgiveness of sins* (Matthew 26:28).

And most unbelievably, in the midst of inconceivable torture at the hands of humans, some of Jesus' final words on the Cross were, *Father, forgive them, they don't know what they are doing* (Luke 23:34).

When we stand in the presence of a perfectly divine Son of God, WE are the ones to quickly say *I'm sorry,* asking for forgiveness and restoration of a broken relationship. Jesus is quick to forgive and restore.

From Grace to Grace:

You seek reconciliation with others by quickly saying, *I'm sorry*, but the ultimate act of *grace* is to say, *Heavenly Father, forgive them because they don't know what they are doing.*

So, by Jesus' example, *Forgive others as you have been forgiven* (Matthew 6:12; Luke 11:4). And when someone sins against you, Jesus instructed us to *forgive, even seventy times seven* (Matthew 18:21-22; Luke 17:3-4).

You have been forgiven by *Grace* so that you can extend the *grace* of forgiveness to others. Essentially, you are saying, *I understand that you are on a journey. Even though you hurt my feelings, I forgive you.* And conversely, you ask for forgiveness and *grace* when you hurt others. *I'm sorry. Please forgive me if I hurt you. I'm on a journey and am grateful for your grace and patience extended to me.*

Bear with each other and forgive one another if any of you have a grievance against someone. Forgive as the Lord forgave you. And over all these virtues put on love, which binds them all together in perfect unity (Colossians 3:12-14)—on and off the dance floor.

A safe place to fail

On the Dance Floor:

The concept that *there are no mistakes in dance* and that *you cannot fail in dance* has some nuances. We all have a filter of what it means to *fail*. There are certain expectations we place on ourselves, especially when competing in dance. It is exciting to get a call-back or to receive a ribbon or award.

We tell ourselves that the accolades aren't the most important part of the journey, but competition adds extra incentive to grow and stretch. In reality, nothing is at stake. I dance as a hobby and a luxury. Dancing is a blessing for this time of life and satisfies the desire of my heart.

But there can be disappointment if I don't achieve an expectation. What happens then? We thrive in an atmosphere where it is safe to be beautiful and to maximize our potential. A *safe place to fail* implies there will be challenges, struggles and disappointments as risks are taken.

When I didn't do as well as expected on the competition floor or didn't get a call back, or receive an award placement that I desired, an atmosphere of *grace* made all the difference in my growth. My pros were quick to speak words that encouraged me to keep moving forward. *I'm proud of you. You danced better than last year. You've worked hard. I know you may be disappointed with the results but remind yourself of how far you've come.*

Dancing with Jesus:

Though Jesus continually calls us to a higher standard—perfection—He doesn't condemn us for our failures during our transformational journey but offers individual course corrections. *Be perfect, therefore, as your heavenly Father is perfect* (Matthew 5:48). For the rich young ruler, his identity was in money which kept him from perfection. Jesus challenged him, *If you want to be perfect, go, sell your possessions and give to the poor, and you will have treasure in heaven. Then come, follow Me* (Matthew 19:21).

A *safe place to fail* while on our journey toward God's standard of perfection is facilitated by an atmosphere that doesn't include shame, guilt or condemnation. Jesus didn't condemn a sinner but challenged her to a higher standard because He loved her and knew that her lifestyle of sin was keeping her from life as He intended—life to the full (John 8:1-11).

Our transformation to perfection as reflected by holiness is made possible only by Jesus. *For by one sacrifice He has made perfect forever those who are being made holy* (Hebrews 10:14).

From Grace to Grace:

You are gracious when you give *grace and space* for people to grow. Their journey probably includes what one might categorize as *failures*—missteps, collisions or major mess-ups. Because you have received and cherish *grace*, you know how much it will mean for those in your sphere to be given encouragement to keep moving when disappointed and disheartened. You can create a safe environment—without shame or condemnation—for others to grow as they continue to move forward.

Grace also includes forgiveness when there are hurts against us—another type of *failure*. You can smile with the realization that each individual is on a journey. By giving *grace and space* you are able to facilitate a person's growth toward potential.

You just need more floor time.

On the Dance Floor:

One of the primary ways to become more confident on the dance floor—especially in competitions—is to take advantage of opportunities to perform before others. The studio continually provided a variety of events for students to showcase their dance journeys in front of familiar faces or at events that were being judged.

It is during *floor time* when experience is gained by sharing dance space and feeling more comfortable while being watched, judged, and critiqued when dancing.

Dancing with Jesus:

Jesus provides an atmosphere of *Grace*—without shame and condemnation—as we progress toward perfection and holiness. Action is required, though. Following His words establishes a foundation and takes time—*floor time*.

Why do you call me, 'Lord, Lord,' and do not do what I say? As for everyone who comes to me and hears my words and puts them into practice, I will show you what they are like. They are like a man building a house, who dug down deep and laid the foundation on rock. When a flood came, the torrent struck that house but could not shake it, because it was well built (Luke 6:46-48).

Jesus was clear about who His followers were: *Those who hear God's word and put it into practice* (Luke 8:21). Following Jesus takes time and practice.

The Apostle Paul understood this and encouraged believers not to sit on the sidelines, but to gain *floor time* through practice. *Whatever you have learned or received or heard from me or seen in me—put it into practice. And the God of peace will be with you* (Philippians 4:9).

From Grace to Grace:

It takes practice and experience to grow a new skill. When you see through the lens of *grace*, you can extend patience when a person doesn't fully demonstrate a newly acquired skill.

Teaching a child a new skill—such as learning to be grateful by saying, *Thank you*—requires consistency and patience and the understanding that with each aspect of growth, *floor time* is required before consistency is achieved. It takes *floor time* before a new skill becomes part of muscle memory or a habit.

I love you.

On the Dance Floor:

At the beginning of a competition, a professional husband and wife team took their position in front of me. While waiting for the music to begin, the woman mouthed the words, *I love you* to her husband-partner. My heart melted, and tears leaked.

Competing professionally has layers of complexity and puts stress on any couple. It is easy to see how the stress could impact a marriage relationship. On the other hand, if the goal is to dance beautifully together as a unit, professional married couples are my favorite dance partnerships to watch. During a performance, married couples seem to add a subtle and genuine level of intimacy to the dance because, in theory, they have an increased level of love for each other.

Through the process of preparation for competition, a married couple has worked as a team and shared the proverbial *blood, sweat, and tears*. On the dance floor, all their hard work is channeled to showcase the couple as a unit, as dancers, and as marriage partners.

Dancing with Jesus:

Intimacy with Jesus is increased when the relationship is not based on fear, but on an understanding of Jesus' heart and a shared vision, passion and missional purpose. Jesus essentially says to us, *I love you; I laid my life down so that we can dance for all eternity together* (John 3:16).

There are numerous examples in the Bible of the relationship between the bridegroom and bride. In Ephesians 5:25-27, husbands are admonished to *love your wives, just as Christ loved the church and gave himself up for her to make her holy.*

The Holy City, the new Jerusalem is described as a beautiful bride (Revelation 21:2) and the wedding of the Lamb (Jesus) and the bride is one of the final demonstrations of the Eternal Love Story (Revelation 19:7, 21:9).

From Grace to Grace:

Dancing from the *head* gives a clean and technical performance. But when a couple dances from a relationship of the *heart*, there is a higher level and expression of intimacy. It mirrors what a marriage should look like off the dance floor—that of a couple working through challenges, setbacks and victories. The ideal marriage relationship is based on love and founded on forgiveness and *grace* where partners genuinely say to each other, *I love you.*

GOLD LEVEL

Those who are dancing at the Gold Level most likely are dancing competitively and showcasing their more advanced skills. The Gold dancer, though mastering foundational levels of Bronze and Silver patterns, typically has developed her or his personal style of dancing. The same dance pattern can be performed by two individuals, and though there will be some similarities, the pattern could look very different because of individual styling, physical ability, how he or she interprets the music, storytelling, and emotional component.

Gold patterns are built on foundational techniques but are more complex, with additional layers of individual styling. There can be Gold-level *closed* routines with patterns specifically from the accepted dance syllabus. Or there can be Gold-level *open* routines with choreography that are created to showcase the individual skill or personality of the dancer. There are no requirements in *open* choreography and the individual and couple are judged on the material presented.

Open routines still include syllabus figures, but there is more flexibility and creativity for the dancer to stylize the routines based on preference.

Hearts beat as one.

On the Dance Floor:

A couple's goal is to dance as if their two hearts beat as one. The first time I danced with Curt in a new partnership, he used the analogy of our two hearts beating as one. The man's heart is the top half of the heart, which pumps blood into the woman's heart. She uses his blood to supply the energy and strength for her to dance beautifully.

As our partnership develops, we are unified through sensitive communication and awareness of our partner, which creates a visual expression of the unity of two individuals dancing as one.

Dancing with Jesus:

When Curt introduced this analogy, I think my heart skipped a beat because he didn't know that I was writing a book about *dancing with Jesus* and all I could think about was *Jesus' blood* that gives me eternal life.

In him we have redemption through his blood, the forgiveness of sins, in accordance with the riches of God's grace (Ephesians 1:7).

This is how we know what love is: Jesus Christ laid down his life for us. And we ought to lay down our lives for our brothers and sisters (1 John 3:16).

From Grace to Grace:

An example of *hearts beating as one* is when a child is developing in her or his mother's womb. The child is literally supported through nutrients in the mother's blood. Though their hearts beat independently and their blood type may be different, physically and emotionally, there is an undeniable connection between the two individuals—mother and baby.

There are times when we sacrifice ourselves—figuratively and literally with *blood, sweat, and tears*—for the benefit of another's growth. This is most pronounced in the relationship between parent and child.

Relationships are connected when you mutually support and love one another. The goal of relationships is to understand one another's heart-to-heart journey and to live in love, harmony, and unity with each other individually and within a community.

How are you doing today?

On the Dance Floor:

Though this question was asked numerous times during my journey, I was able to process the importance and impact of the question more specifically with Curt. During one of my first coaching sessions with him, he asked me how I was doing, and I replied that I was actually doing very well that day. Then I explained that when I was a Newcomer at the studio and was asked that same question, tears would well up. Why?

I was in a season of responding to the emotional and physical needs of numerous people in my sphere of influence. When a person would ask *me* how I was doing, tears would well up because it showed that someone cared about *me*. There is a difference between *What did you do today?* (seen through a filter of performance-orientation) and *How are you doing today?*

Once I processed the concept of addressing the condition of *my* heart with Curt, he made sure that at the beginning of every dance session he asked that very important question to check in with how my heart was doing. Then he listened as I could authentically share the status of my heart.

Dancing with Jesus:

Jesus was, and is, the Master of emphasizing the status of our hearts. He came to heal the brokenhearted, to comfort, to restore our soul, to set us free (Luke 4:18-21). Yes, He has commissioned us to *do,* to use our talents and serve others (Matthew 25:14-30), but sometimes we forget that He said, *Come to Me, all who are weary and burdened, and rest* (Matthew 11:28). He gives permission to rest from *doing* and just *be.* Be with Him and rest in Him.

Numerous times, Jesus addressed the condition of a person's heart and interacted with people at the heart level. He understood that how we are doing emotionally has an impact on how we relate to others (Matthew 15:19). As I surrender the condition of my heart to Jesus and rest and *dance with Him*, I am renewed, transformed, and able to love others more fully through Him.

From Grace to Grace:

Experiencing the *grace* of being seen and valued for *who you are* as a person—not solely on *what you do* for someone—has life-changing effects on relationships. You can look people in their eyes with *grace* and inquire as to the status of their hearts. You can prioritize helping others in their journey of wholeness, restoring broken hearts, and comforting and encouraging others to pursue joy, peace, and freedom in a heart relationship with Jesus.

Be you!

On the Dance Floor:

Dance with your own style. There are various personality styles that play out on the dance floor. Two people can dance the same pattern, but with unique and individual styles. A continuum of styles includes sassy to sensual, with different interpretations of music and patterns.

While I desire to dance more *freely*—sometimes comparing my *safe* personality to another's *free* expression—I'm grateful to be given encouragement from my instructors to *Be you!* I am learning to dance with the freest version of me that expresses who I uniquely am at a specific moment in my life's journey.

Dancing with Jesus:

From conception, each one of us is uniquely created with individual personalities, gifts, and talents.

You are the one who put me together inside my mother's body, and I praise You because of the wonderful way You created me. Everything You do is marvelous! Of this I have no doubt! I was secretly woven together out of human sight, but with Your own eyes you saw my body being formed.

Even before I was born, You had written in Your book everything about me (Psalm 139:13-16).

Jesus delights in every one of His creations. While He walked on the earth, He related to each individual based on his or her unique personhood. He addressed people according to his or her needs and personality. To some, He spoke with tenderness; to others, He challenged. Each encounter was specific to the individual because Jesus understood his or her heart condition and personal journey.

From Grace to Grace:

Each person has been created with a unique personality and a wide range of talents and desires. You can give *grace* by extending freedom for others to express their individuality. You will find joy in watching a person discover and showcase his or herself and admire the impact made on the world because of who he or she uniquely is.

There is freedom in the lead.

On the Dance Floor:

As a woman becomes more experienced with dance technique, steps and patterns and is more confident in her abilities and performance, she is more comfortable to dance within the framework of the lead that is given. As a particular pattern is led by her partner, she can make choices regarding arm styling and presentation within the sequence. Her partner provides a consistent frame, communicates effectively, and creates space for her to embellish with her personal dance style.

Dancing with Jesus:

As an individual grows in his or her relationship with Jesus, the level of trust, safety and freedom is communicated from the *frame* and *lead* of Jesus. At this stage in the journey with Jesus, an individual senses the commission of Jesus to *Go, make disciples of nations, baptize and teach* (Matthew 28:19-20) and understands that it is accompanied with the freedom to move in his or her unique personality and gifting.

While still connected to Jesus and listening to His communication, His followers is free to follow the *lead* and *embellish* with choices that are individual to his or her personal journey with Jesus.

1 Corinthians 12 describes a variety of gifts of the Spirit that include teaching, wisdom, healing, prophecy, administration, and other aspects of helping. As Jesus says, *Go;* there is confidence and freedom in His *lead* even as we are sent out with unique gifting. *Grace* smiles on the individual as he or she moves into the world, reflecting Jesus' Love through gifts of His Spirit.

From Grace to Grace:

When an individual is confident in his or her unique gifting that has been forged from *dancing with Jesus*, it is fulfilling to assist others in identifying their own gifts and talents and watch them *dance with Jesus* as a one-of-a-kind creation.

You can cheer others on, admire their unique *embellishment,* and marvel at how Jesus connects, communicates, and dances with each one of us as He sends us out into the world to impact others with His heart of Love.

Experienced dancers know how to wait.

On the Dance Floor:

As a dancer becomes familiar and comfortable with the pace of the music, he or she can learn to breathe and not rush the steps. It seems the music actually becomes *slower*. This is just a perception, though. The music has not changed—it is just that the dancer has learned how to *wait* and fill each section of a beat.

As a dancer learns to *wait*—not rushing the movement but enjoying the entire length of a beat—there is a flow that is breathtaking to observe. A woman trustingly waits for the Leader to initiate the movement, which means she is slightly behind the beat of the music. It might seem counterintuitive to dance slightly behind the beat, but the overall picture is one of unity. The body flows, breathes, and fills each moment before rushing to the next step.

Dancing with Jesus:

As a follower of Jesus spends more time dancing with Him, he or she grows in trust—in following Jesus' lead and listening for the communication signals that are given through the connection. Because the follower has grown in trust in Jesus, he or she has learned to *wait* for the next lead, not rushing ahead of the lead in the direction or rhythm of the relationship.

Psalm 37:7 is one of my favorite scriptures. A combination of various Bible versions reminds me to *be still and silent before the Lord. Wait patiently and expectantly for Him.* I choose to be still and silent before the Lord, waiting patiently and expectantly for His lead. I'm listening intently to read His communication, resting in the present moment and eagerly waiting expectantly to see where He will lead in the next phase of the journey.

From Grace to Grace:

When you move through life filled with *grace* and trust, there is an ease and peacefulness of movement. A person who knows how to *wait* has a settling effect on those around him or her. A *gracious* person does not communicate striving, pressing, pushing, rushing, or impatience. Instead, the *graceful* person has a presence of breathful anticipation and patience for what life will bring while enjoying the present moment of every day or season in life.

Dance is a lifelong journey.

On the Dance Floor:

It is inspiring for me to see men and women who are well up in years—*older*—who continue to step onto the dance floor, whether for social dance, for instruction, or to compete. It is as if they HAVE to dance—it is who they are—even though they are not able to physically move to the same level as when *younger*.

Watching a lifelong dancer confirms that he or she dances from the heart, long after the time the body was able to respond with more physicality. The dancer may be holding more closely to his or her dance partner or instructor, with movement limited. For those of us still in the pursuit of continual growth, the message is an encouraging one—keep dancing! The journey of a lifetime continues.

I have realized that I dance because it is who I am. I'm a dancer. God created me with the desire to grow and experience life through the medium of dance. Because of that, my dance journey will continue until my final days. Music moves me emotionally and physically.

The encouragement to continue with my growth process has come from the kind words and actions of my professional coaches. They, too, are dancers and continue in their growth journey by continuing to be coached, to grow, and to compete.

And just as there are seasons in my life, professional dancers also have seasons in their dance journey. There comes a time when they retire from more active forms of competition, and some step into additional roles as coaches, mentors, and judges. Their role continues to be one of passing along their expertise gained through the years.

Dancing with Jesus:

As we age, we may not have the same energy or physical ability to minister and serve others as before. Our reality is that *though the spirit is willing, the flesh is weak* (Matthew 26:41). But because of our relationship with Jesus, we still have the same focus to serve Him and we move into different seasons of mentoring and encouraging others.

No matter our circumstances, we are all on a lifelong journey with Jesus. Apostle Paul wrote, *I press on to take hold of that for which Christ Jesus took hold of me . . . Forgetting what is behind and straining toward what is ahead . . .* (Philippians 3:12-13).

However, I consider my life worth nothing to me; my only aim is to finish the race and complete the task the Lord Jesus has given me—the task of testifying to the good news of God's grace (Acts 20:24).

We look forward to the *renewal of all things* (Matthew 19:28), including our bodies. Until then, just as Jesus came to *serve and not to be served* (Mark 10:45), we follow His lead into eternity.

From Grace to Grace:

Just as Jesus served, we are tasked with mentoring and encouraging others physically and spiritually, especially those in the earlier phases of their journeys. We never *age out* of our role to serve others.

Each of you should use whatever gift you have received to serve others as faithful stewards of God's grace in its various forms (1 Peter 4:10).

Release

On the Dance Floor:

Because my personality is more guarded and cautious—maybe even timid—when combined with the emphasis on dance posture and frame, I tend to dance in control and somewhat constricted. My heart says to *let go* and dance freely, but my body says to dance *safely.*

How does a dancer combine the strength of muscle control with a release of muscles to dance freely? It may seem counterintuitive and impossible, but through the progression of my dance journey, I realize that learning to release myself physically and emotionally will help me dance more fully.

Dancing with Jesus:

One of the most profound encounters Jesus had with a crippled woman was initiated with His words, *You are set free! Jesus then placed His hands on her and she straightened up and praised God.* Jesus told the crowd that Satan bound this woman for eighteen years and it gave Him great pleasure to release her from the bondage she had endured (Luke 13:10-17).

The common theme of Jesus' life and ministry is that He came to *save, redeem and restore* to wholeness and fullness—to set us free to *live life fully* (John 10:10). Jesus released us from spiritual and physical bonds so that we would be released to share the Good News of Him with the whole world.

From Grace to Grace:

When you are set free and released from the physical, spiritual, and emotional constraints that bind or restrict you, there is confidence to go out and live out your purpose and destiny more fully. That destiny and purpose is to go and share the Good News about Jesus' desire for eternal wholeness.

Can you say that you have been set free from constraints that inhibit or restrict your ability to live life to the full? What might you need to release in order to dance and live more fully? Be courageous, dear Reader!

The student reflects the quality of instruction received.

On the Dance Floor:

When competing, a student is evaluated for his or her skill level. But at higher levels of competition, the individual is judged in relation to the dance partnership. The student will absorb the teaching emphasis and style of the teacher and reflect the instruction of his or her coach. It is important, therefore, that the student seek an instructor who not only is skilled and perfecting his or her craft but also has the ability to translate that knowledge to the student in the relevant application so that growth is apparent.

As I progressed in my dance ability, it was important to seek instructors who were more experienced so that my growth trajectory would continue.

Dancing with Jesus:

The Master Teacher—Jesus—said, *Come learn from Me. Take My yoke upon you and learn from Me, for I am gentle and lowly in heart, and you will find rest for your souls* (Matthew 11:29).

A disciple is not above his teacher, but everyone who is perfectly trained will be like his teacher (Luke 6:40 NKJV).

I in them, and You in Me; that they may be made perfect in one, and that the world may know that You have sent Me and have loved them as You have loved Me (John 17:23 NKJV).

When we dance with Jesus, we know that we are learning from the Master Teacher who modeled perfection and was an exact replication of His Father in heaven (John 14:9-10; Colossians 1:15). Our spiritual goal is to *be conformed to the image of God's Son*, reflecting His qualities (Romans 8:29).

From Grace to Grace:

Because we learn from those we associate with, it is important that you surround yourself with quality people who positively influence your life journey and relationship with God. As you yourself are becoming perfected to represent Your Master Teacher, you model and pass that legacy to those around you—primarily to the next generation.

It is an honor and profound responsibility to become teachers and coaches in passing along life lessons, guiding younger ones, and introducing them to the Master Teacher—Jesus—who is the only Perfect One who provides the way to eternity.

She's my student.

On the Dance Floor:

When a visiting coach complimented me on my growth, my instructor, John, made the comment that it gave him great pride to acknowledge that I was one of his students. It brought him joy knowing that his student had taken his instruction and consistently applied it over the course of time and that I was beginning to reflect positively on his ability as a teacher and mentor. And it brought me great joy that he delighted in me, his student.

Dancing with Jesus:

During Jesus' final prayer before His trial, He thanked His Father for *those you have given Me* and prayed for their protection after He was glorified (John 17:1-18). Previously, Jesus told His disciples, *I no longer call you servants but call you friends* (John 15:15).

As we dance with Him, trusting Him as His disciples did, He calls us friends. The Master Teacher delights in presenting His friends before His Father, knowing that over time, we are reflecting His nature and character and are being transformed by Him.

In the analogy of a sheep's relationship with the Shepherd, Jesus stated, *My sheep listen to my voice; I know them, and they follow me. I give them eternal life, and they shall never perish; no one will snatch them out of my hand. My Father, who has given them to me, is greater than all; no one can snatch them out of my Father's hand* (John 10:27-29).

Though Jesus ascended to heaven after His death and resurrection, our relationship with Him continues through His Spirit. *Because Jesus lives forever, He has a permanent priesthood. Therefore, He is able to completely save those who come to God through Him, because He always lives to intercede for them* (Hebrews 7:24-25).

From Grace to Grace:

As you pour yourself into the development of others by teaching, encouraging, and providing growth opportunities, it gives you great joy and a sense of pride when you see them thrive and succeed in life. Even through difficulties and challenges, your persistence and loyalty convey that you are committed to a person's victories and are grateful to play an important part in their life's journey.

Don't anticipate the lead.

On the Dance Floor:

As a dancer moves from the beginner level, there is encouragement to dance more independently. This higher level of dance also comes with the challenge to continue listening to physical cues from the Leader, even while dancing more independently.

Even though I might know the steps and choreography, I am reminded not to anticipate what the Leader will do. There will be times when he needs to change direction because of navigating the dance floor. I must let the Leader lead and then react to his communication.

There will be a richer dance partnership and expression when my body reacts to the direction of the Leader instead of anticipating what I think he is going to do. Learning to dance in the present, though difficult, displays an intentionally focused and relaxed performance.

Dancing with Jesus:

Because we only have a limited perspective, our human proclivity is to make decisions based on what we see immediately without waiting to hear clearly from Jesus. Don't anticipate Jesus' lead. He sees more clearly to navigate our journey. Wait for Him to show what direction, what the next step is, and how quickly to move. This takes a consistent and growing trust in the Master Teacher and Leader.

Don't worry about tomorrow for tomorrow will worry about itself. Each day has enough trouble of its own (Matthew 6:34).

Submit plans to Him, then trust Him to lead. *Trust in the LORD with all your heart and lean not on your own understanding* (Proverbs 3:5).

When we live in the present, trusting Him to lead, we will dance peacefully through life. *You will keep in perfect peace those whose minds are steadfast because they trust in You* (Isaiah 26:3).

From Grace to Grace:

You can help others live more fully in the moment—in the present—instead of over-emphasizing what might happen in the future. It is counterproductive to worry about tomorrow because we have no control over the future.

One of the greatest gifts you can offer those around you is to model trust in Jesus and wait patiently and expectantly for Him to communicate the next step or direction in life. A person living in the present and trusting God with the future exudes a sense of peace that is contagious.

The Follower keeps inviting the Lead.

On the Dance Floor:

The Follower (me) *needs to keep inviting the Lead* (my Pro). What?!! When this phrase was spoken, I had to stop and ask for clarification. One of the first lessons as a Newcomer emphasized that the Leader invites the Follower to dance, and her role is to follow. But this new phrase implied mutuality, equality and independence of roles.

As my instructor explained this phrase, it became more clear. When in a closed frame, it was now my role to keep inviting the Leader into my space as I was moving backward in *go* mode. The Leader would rather me have a stronger response (invitation) than lapses in connection. The more that I move and keep *inviting* the lead, the greater the ability, distance, and power we have as a couple.

Dancing with Jesus:

Initially, Jesus invites me to dance with Him, but my role is to keep the connection, to keep moving in the direction that He has asked me to go. Once He says, *Go*, I *go*, inviting Him through my connection to stay involved in the dance.

When reading John 6 about a controversial teaching of Jesus, many of His disciples turned away. Jesus asked Peter if he wanted to leave, too. *Lord, to whom shall we go? You have the words of eternal life. We have come to believe and to know that you are the Holy One of God* (John 6:66-69).

The journey with Jesus is challenging. But where else would I go? He alone is the Holy One of God, with words of eternal life. *Jesus alone is the Way and the Truth and the Life. No one can come to the Father except through Him* (John 14:6).

It is more beneficial in the long run to stay consistently connected instead of having lapses in communication. The end result of our partnership is more effective, fuller, and dynamic if I consistently stay connected and embrace my role of inviting Him to dance. Jesus and I dance together. He trusts me to *go,* and we develop dependence, independence, and mutuality of dance.

The optimal relationship is to stay connected. But Jesus is patient and *graciously* forgives even when we don't stay connected or have lapses in our dance with Him.

I tell Jesus that no matter what, I choose to stay connected to Him and that I *am always with You; You hold me by my right hand. You guide me with Your counsel, and afterward You will take me into glory* (Psalm 73:23-24).

From Grace to Grace:

Relationships develop when both individuals are mutually and equally invested in the relationship. Two are greater than one, but the depth of the relationship is increased when both individuals use strength, passion, and commitment to consistently stay connected.

In dancing, there are times when the Leader is in *stop* or *go* mode. And there are times when the Follower is in *stop* or *go* mode. There is an ebb and flow of responsibilities, creating the continuity of movement and a dynamic dance. Similarly, when a relationship is mutual, independent, dependent, and connected, there is genuine strength that is beautiful to watch.

Permission granted

On the Dance Floor:

Even after four amazing years into my dance journey, and even though I've made huge progress in the physical, mental, and emotional growth aspects of dance, I consciously and subconsciously still battle some of the core issues I brought into the studio on my first lesson. One of my instructors was observing my lesson and asked if he could share his insights. *I can't quite figure out what is holding you back. You dance 'pretty', but it seems safe and comfortable. It's as if you are still asking for permission to dance out of your comfort zone.*

Permission. Initially, I wasn't sure what it was about the word *permission*, but it jumped out at me. I paused, then began to tear up. Yes, *permission* was where I continued to stall in my journey. I've made huge strides in dancing less afraid, less timid and restricted. But I know intuitively that I'm still stuck. *Permission.* Even though there are still traces of a lack of support and lifelong ceilings that I use as an excuse to limit myself, I need to give myself *permission* to dance more freely and fully.

Courageously, I gave my instructor permission—again—to continue to stretch me out of my *safe and comfortable* dance style. He assured me that even though the challenge would mean I would dance more *messy* (not perfect), he would support me because the ultimate goal is to dance more fully and freely.

Dancing with Jesus:

Permission. Jesus already invited me into the dance—*Will you dance with Me?*—and by my acceptance and surrender to the process of dancing freely and fully with Him, permission was granted. He gave me permission to become the best version of me that He had created. And I had given Him permission to lead the process of restoration into wholeness.

Here I am! I stand at the door and knock. If anyone hears My voice and opens the door, I will come in and eat with that person, and they with Me (Revelation 3:20).

Jesus asks. He knocks. He invites, never imposing Himself. Permission to enter is granted. And once He has been invited into the relationship, it becomes mutual and we grant Him permission to be our Leader, navigating our dance journey with Him.

From Grace to Grace:

Grace essentially says to someone, *I give you permission to become the best version of you that is possible.* The journey will be messy and unpredictable—maybe even a bit wild—and will require loyalty, patience, endurance, and forgiveness during the process. But when relationships are built upon a foundation and gift of *grace*—not control or expectations of performance—true freedom is granted for an individual to grow and thrive.

I just want to dance!

On the Dance Floor:

The first entry in this book recounted my response to why I was interested in taking ballroom dance lessons. *I just NEED to dance!* Over four years of consistent lessons and progression of skills, I began to feel disheartened, maybe even discouraged. Yes, I made huge progress in all areas of dance, but there was still an underlying message of *not being good enough,* and *more* was required of me.

Because I have chosen to showcase my dance ability on the competition floor, lessons are intentionally challenging, and I'm grateful for my path. But frequently, I now find myself so much in my head with the endless jumble of mental notes—frame up, head weight, connect, heel lead, don't anticipate, stay grounded, extend, expression, drive, release, etc.—that at times I become numb and lose enjoyment of the dance. I'm back in my head, limiting myself again, but now at a higher level.

Sometimes, *I just want to DANCE!* I just want to turn on the music and move to the expression of the rhythm, mood, and phrasing of the music. No choreography, no statements or corrections from my instructor, no *notes to self*—just dance. Pure, lovely, uncomplicated, and free dance.

Dancing with Jesus:

I believe Jesus understood the meaning of the phrase *I just want to dance!* I can only imagine the continual pressure and tugs on His time and attention. That is why He prioritized time alone with His Father without all the lovely *noise* of humanity in His ears.

Very early in the morning, while it was still dark, Jesus got up, left the house and went off to a solitary place, where he prayed (Mark 1:35). His source of strength came from time with His Father. Though Jesus was always one with His Father (John 17), He intentionally took time away from the human expectations and realities of His journey to be refreshed.

It is encouraging for me that Jesus invites me to *dance with Him*—alone. *Come to Me, all of you who are weary and heavy burdened, and I will give you rest* (Matthew 11:28). Jesus invited His disciples to *come with Me by yourselves to a quiet place and get some rest* (Mark 6:31).

As you probably know by now, I love the heart of Mary of Bethany, one of Jesus' closest friends. She just longed to be with Him, choosing to sit at His feet and learn from Him. He affirmed her choice and gave her permission to rest with and in Him (Luke 10:38-42). Her *dance with Jesus* was uncomplicated and refreshing for both. She could just be herself, rest, and cherish every moment in His presence.

From Grace to Grace:

Though a large part of our human journey includes doing, learning, growing, and moving forward, there are times when you need to give yourself and others the necessity of *rest* and *being*. It is important in your relationships to allow space to breathe, to play, and to set time away from your lists, goals, and projects to be refreshed spiritually, physically, emotionally, and mentally.

Each person has his or her own place of *being*. You can encourage those closest to you by validating the important aspect of humanity—our *being*, out of which comes our *doing* when revived and refreshed.

I'm so happy for you!

On the Dance Floor:

One of the students who earned numerous awards and accolades during her dance journey was so excited for me when I placed third in a competition. She watched me progress from beginner to placing in the finals and responded with shouts of enthusiasm when I had a victory.

Her celebration of my accomplishment—though she won many first-place ribbons—was genuine and made me feel welcomed and affirmed.

As the two of us progressed in our dance ability, there would be numerous times when we would be competing *against* each other. Though challenging at first, another aspect of my personal growth was to give genuine congratulations and be happy when she and others placed higher than I did.

I also learned to receive compliments, resisting the tendency to compare my dancing with another.

Dancing with Jesus:

. . . there should be no division in the body, but that its parts should have equal concern for each other. If one part suffers, every part suffers with it; if one part is honored, every part rejoices with it. Now you are the body of Christ, and each one of you is a part of it (1 Corinthians 12:25-27).

2 Corinthians 10:12 provides the principle that *it is not wise to compare oneself with another.* Thankfully, Jesus does not compare our spiritual journey with another. We can truly be happy to witness the victories of others.

From Grace to Grace:

When you have been celebrated for your victories, no matter how small, you know how encouraging it can be. Therefore, remember to encourage others, even if it may seem that they are your competitors. You can remind yourself and others that we are on individual journeys and not in competition or comparing with them. That is *grace.*

I'm reminding you that you said 'yes'.

On the Dance Floor:

In a moment of courage, I messaged my instructor, John, and admitted that I realized that to become the dancer I envisioned included accepting opportunities to perform. So bravely, I said *yes* to performing a solo in the upcoming theater show. But the closer the time came to perform; I had increasing self-doubts and threw out several excuses as to why I didn't want to perform. *Barb, it would be easier to say 'no', but I'm reminding you that you said 'yes' to opportunities to grow into the dancer you know you can be. There is no pressure with the performance. Just be you and dance from your heart because you love to dance.*

Thankfully, I had a partner who gently convinced me not to lose heart. He reminded me that saying *no* would be the easier route to take, but saying *yes* would be more beneficial for my long-term heart journey.

Dancing with Jesus:

Grace takes away performance mentality and the pressure of pleasing others, even Jesus. I *dance with Jesus* because I love to dance with Him. Yes, there are challenges and struggles, and at times, it might seem easier to take a break or walk away. But Jesus gently reminds us that we will be victorious because He is victorious.

I have told you these things, so that in me you may have peace. In this world you will have trouble. But take heart! I have overcome the world (John 16:33).

Jesus also reminds us to honor our commitments, especially to Him. *No one who puts a hand to the plow and looks back is fit for service in the kingdom of God* (Luke 9:62). This statement may seem harsh, but when we trust Jesus with our journey—even through the troubles—we do not have to be afraid.

From Grace to Grace:

You can remind and encourage others to continue on their growth path. Yes, there are challenges, but the ultimate goal in life is to grow in ability and maximize our gifts and talents—not to please others or to earn another person's approval, but to honor the Creator Who gave us the gifts, talents, and passion to pursue our unique calling.

People are rewarded for what they practice in private.

On the Dance Floor:

While watching the 2018 final of *The World of Dance,* I was struck by a phrase spoken by Derek Hough, a judge, and contemporary dance icon, when he was mentoring a pair of young women dancing on the world stage for the first time. They were unknowns from a small town but had a passion for dance and were committed to perfecting their craft. Their investment of time and money over many years, practicing and continually challenging themselves, reaped an abundance of accolades and respect during this significant competition. Derek reminded them that they were being *rewarded for what they had been practicing for years in private.*

Though I didn't begin my dance journey with the intent of going *public,* Derek's statement encouraged me. My dance journey is private, taking place in the dance studio where only a few people are witnesses. Because of the consistency of my commitment to develop over the years, when I do perform on a competition floor, there is an increasing recognition for my accomplishments. That's not the reason I dance, but it is affirming when progress is publicly acknowledged.

Dancing with Jesus:

Be careful not to practice your righteousness in front of others to be seen by them. If you do, you will have no reward from your Father in heaven. So when you give to the needy, do not announce it with trumpets, as the hypocrites do in the synagogues and on the streets, to be honored by others. Truly, I tell you, they have received their reward in full. But when you give to the needy, do not let your left hand know what your right hand is doing so that your giving may be in secret. Then your Father, who sees what is done in secret, will reward you.

And when you pray, do not be like the hypocrites, for they love to pray standing in the synagogues and on the street corners to be seen by others. Truly I tell you, they have received their reward in full. But when you pray, go into your room, close the door and pray to your Father, who is unseen. Then your Father, who sees what is done in secret, will reward you (Matthew 6:1-6).

Our spiritual relationship with God primarily takes place in private through a consistent dialogue of prayer and meditation on His Word. The transformation of a person's heart through the indwelling of God's Spirit takes time and is driven by a passion to follow Jesus and become more like Him. The relationship is intimately private, though the overflow of the transformation becomes increasingly apparent for the world to witness.

From Grace to Grace:

Grace recognizes and responds to the transformation of the humble. The majority of individuals lead simple and private lives, unassumingly influencing others in their spheres. Parents, caregivers, and teachers need to be affirmed that their service does make a difference.

When you understand that your relationship with God develops with personal and private time in communion with Jesus, you can encourage others to value their solo time with God.

You are capable of more than you think.

On the Dance Floor:

After a dance competition in which I did relatively well, I intuitively knew that I was capable of even more. But I also felt constrained, not knowing how to move my body more fully. I needed to feel the movement. After the competition, I had a coaching session with Marina, one of the judges. Though she didn't know me, she commented, *I can tell there is more in you, that your body has the ability to do more . . . you are capable of more than you think.*

Then she proceeded to physically move my body by pulling my left shoulder down and back while stretching my right rib cage upward, then rotating the entire upper body. Tug, pull, stretch.

Do you feel that? Let's try it again . . . that's right, left shoulder down and back, stretch, more . . . can you feel that? Actually, it was so helpful to feel what my body was capable of. If I couldn't grasp a new step or movement, I would ask my coach to help me feel how my body was supposed to move.

Dancing with Jesus:

Only Jesus knows His plan for us and our potential. He also understands the growth and stretch that is necessary to reach our fullest destiny. Surrender to His capable hands. Trust that He knows best and that He has your best interest at heart. Any stretch, pruning, or refining from Him can be trusted. He is faithful and knows that within the pruning process, the result is to bear more fruit, bringing glory to the Father.

I am the true vine, and my Father is the gardener. He cuts off every branch in me that bears no fruit, while every branch that does bear fruit He prunes so that it will be even more fruitful (John 15:1-2).

So, in surrender and trust, I have learned to say, *Here I am. Send me!* Gulp! It will be a challenge, but I trust that He will be there pulling and tugging with strong yet gentle hands.

From Grace to Grace:

One of the greatest roles you can play in the lives of others is as an encourager. *I believe in you . . . you have what it takes . . . you are capable of more than you think . . . I see it in you . . . you can do it. Go!*

When a person is in the midst of a challenge or trial, it is difficult to see a bigger picture of where she or he is headed or the long-term benefit of the struggle. *Grace* encourages and helps the individual look ahead at the blessing and victory.

I want to brighten your day.

On the Dance Floor:

My instructor, Bella, shared how grateful she is for our sessions because I brighten her day. Instead of complaining or making excuses, I come with a courageous attitude, willing to listen and try whatever is asked of me.

As a teacher myself, I understand the joy of having a willing and receptive student in contrast to a grumbling, unmotivated one. One of my current joys is interacting with my first grandson. He brightens my day because every moment of every day he is naturally soaking up all the experiences that we call *learning.* To him, it is just *living* and *playing,* and it brings me great joy to teach him and expose him to everything new.

That is how I want to approach dance. Every day is a new learning opportunity—full of discoveries, adventures, creativity, and joy. It makes me happy to know that my instructors look forward to our lessons together because I love learning. Even though each session challenges me greatly, I find immeasurable joy in my dance journey.

Dancing with Jesus:

Jesus proclaimed: *I am the light of the world. Anyone who follows Me will never walk in the darkness but will have the light of life* (John 8:12).

Not only is Jesus light, but when we follow Him, we reflect His light. *So, our faces are not covered. They show the bright glory of the Lord, as the Lord's Spirit makes us more and more like our glorious Lord* (2 Corinthians 3:18). Jesus' light shines with His bright glory of joy.

Jesus' apostles wrote about the joy that we have when following Him. Paul expressed his commitment to stay with the believers in Philippi so that they would mature in their faith and have joy in it (Philippians 1:25). Apostle John expressed, *I have no greater joy than to hear that my children are walking in the truth* (3 John 1:4).

The author of Hebrews encouraged those in the church to *have confidence in your leaders and submit to their authority . . . so that their work will be a joy, not a burden* (Hebrews 13:17).

From Grace to Grace:

For those of us who have the privilege of being a teacher, we understand how delightful it is to have a student who genuinely wants to learn from our teaching. An eager student is curious and responsive, in contrast to an obstinate student who doesn't want to be in class, who thinks he or she knows it all, or who is not motivated to do what it takes to grow. What joy and encouragement it is for a teacher to be respected and appreciated for the role played in the life of a student.

When you are in a learner situation—such as in a work setting, conference, or recipient of coaching or mentoring—you can express respect and appreciation for the efforts of the teacher because you understand the difference between an eager and unresponsive student.

I feel the most free when I am dancing.

On the Dance Floor:

The dance staff finally convinced me to perform a routine in the annual Theater Show. My partner had previously reminded me that I said *yes*. While waiting in the wings in anticipation of my performance, I began sharing with professional dancer Melanie my journey and stated that this was an *act of courage* in an attempt to overcome my timidity. I intentionally chose to dance a dynamic tango to a victorious song by Muse.

Melanie stated that she had been dancing since she was three years old and felt the most free when dancing on stage in the lights or in competition. I certainly admired her ability to dance freely. Her energy and joy were inspiring and contagious.

I dance because it is the vehicle toward making me more free, confident, and fully alive. In my process of dancing, I anticipate that one day, I, too, will feel the most free when I am dancing.

Dancing with Jesus:

After accepting the invitation to dance with Jesus and learning to stay connected and follow His lead, I can truly say that I feel the most free when in His presence. No matter what human circumstances are swirling around me, as long as I intentionally prioritize my relationship with Jesus, I face the day with joy and peace. *You are set free. Live life to the full.*

Freedom comes from trust. My relationship with Jesus is the most trustworthy and pure relationship because only He is true and pure and has my best interests at heart. I am my truest, most authentic self when *dancing with Jesus*.

Therefore, having been justified by faith, we have peace with God through our Lord Jesus Christ, through whom also we have access by faith into this grace in which we stand, and rejoice in hope of the glory of God (Romans 5:1-2).

From Grace to Grace:

Just as Melanie's glowing presence on the dance floor was inspiring and contagious, when you share with others what makes you feel most free, it is encouraging for them. What is the avenue or area where you feel most fully free and alive—most fully who God created you to be? Is that when you are painting, designing a landscape, or teaching a child to read? When are you singing or hiking in the mountains?

More importantly, have you accepted the invitation to a relationship with Jesus? It is only within that relationship you will feel and be fully and eternally free. You can encourage others to keep pursuing freedom—freedom from fear, guilt, and shame. More importantly, encourage others in their *dance with Jesus*. Their relationship with Jesus is ultimately the only place they will feel and be eternally free.

Celebrate!

On the Dance Floor:

All is well. At the end of a competition event, there is typically a celebration dinner, with feasting, dancing, flowers and awards presentations. The challenges of the event are over. Any internal struggles with fear, comparisons, self-doubts and disappointments are in the rear-view mirror. A few tears of frustration may have been shed and participants are exhausted from physically stretching and performing beyond what was thought possible. Maybe there are slight injuries from getting stepped on, but now it is time to rejoice and celebrate with fellow dancers.

Dancing with Jesus:

Just as Jesus faced challenges during His life—and especially with His final act on the cross—when it was finished, He rejoiced. *For the joy set before Him He endured the cross . . . and sat down at the right hand of the throne of God* (Hebrews 12:2). Jesus knew that our journey on earth would not be easy and used the analogy of a woman giving birth—with travail—but with joy at the birth of a child (John 16:21).

1 Corinthians 2:9 says that *we cannot even conceive of what the Lord has in store for those who love Him.* When Jesus returns, *He will reward each person according to what they have done* (Matthew 16:27). We also know that *those who are invited to the wedding supper of the Lamb are blessed* (Revelation 19:6-9).

There will be rejoicing at the wedding celebration of the Lamb, Jesus. I envision feasting, dancing, and sharing memories with loved ones. The end of this part of the story is finished and there will be no more death, mourning or pain (Revelation 21:4), only an eternity of joy.

Let them praise His name with the dance; Let them sing praises to Him with the timbrel and harp (Psalm 149:3).

From Grace to Grace:

The times you celebrate on earth are a foretaste of the celebration in heaven. Festive occasions are a reminder that in the end the pain, the struggle and the challenges will all be worth it.

You did it! You overcame and long to hear Jesus say, *Well done! I'm proud of you! Here is your reward!*

You took my breath away.

On the Dance Floor:

The first time I saw the professional married couple Nicolae Colac and Bella Gubzheva dance was during a dinner showcase at the completion of a competition weekend. Bella had previously given me additional coaching during several lessons. I learned that she had won international competitions which was no surprise because she danced at a level most would never experience. I had seen Nicolae at another competition and knew Bella and he were professional partners, but had never seen them dance together.

Oh my . . . I can't even begin to describe what the audience witnessed when they began their rumba routine. We sat mesmerized by the level of skill, unity, and showmanship presented.

Then the music stopped . . . and they continued dancing in perfect synchronization. I think my heart actually stopped beating, and I don't think I took a breath. Then the music began again, but they really didn't need music. Their dance was beyond stunning, and I knew that I had witnessed a true dance partnership.

Dancing with Jesus:

When reading the stories of how Jesus interacted with the women and men He encountered, there are numerous times when I am captured by His magnificence, and it takes my breath away. His *Grace* and ability to speak targeted words of truth in every situation is stunning. I try to put myself into the sandals of the recipients of His touch or those who were able to witness the scenario He was orchestrating. Jesus truly was and is divine, even while walking on earth as a human.

I'm profoundly impacted by Jesus' powerful and kind nature. He healed the blind, deaf, and crippled. He cast out demons, rescued, confronted, and restored—all with an ease and *Grace* that seemed effortless. Jesus was so assured of who He was—the beloved Son of God—and in perfect unity with His Father that He walked on the earth in ways that leave me mesmerized and marveling at His glorious and indescribable *Grace*.

What will it be like at the end of time to witness the heavenly throne of God? If the angels and elders and living creatures fall down on their faces and worship God, we will also. The beauty and majesty of God will be breathtaking, and we will bow in adoration (Revelation 7:11, 19:4) because of the *incomparable riches of His Grace* (Ephesians 2:6-10).

From Grace to Grace:

You can experience the *grace* of *dancing with Jesus* while here on earth, but your ultimate hope lies in *dancing with Jesus* at the end of time when all things will be made new and there will be no more death or sorrow (Revelation 21, 22).

While you wait expectantly, be thankful for those glimpses into heaven when your heart seems to stop beating and you witness something that takes your breath away. What are glimmers of *grace* that are a breathtaking taste of heaven? Hearing a newborn cry, enjoying the joyful giggle of a child, observing a sunset, listening to a symphony or tasting a fine wine? These are gifts of *grace*.

I want to listen to one voice.

On the Dance Floor:

My journey with ballroom dance began in 2013 in the Arthur Murray Costa Mesa studio and has continued uninterrupted up to this entry. It seems appropriate that my final experience with AM was during a time of celebration at my biggest annual competition. Because of my journey in the AM studio, I am no longer afraid to step onto the dance floor and am confident in my dance abilities. So much so that I'm choosing to focus on the coaching of the one woman instructor whom I want to dance like. Bella briefly coached me in the AM studio, and when she moved to another studio, I knew that it was time for me to focus and submit to the instruction and guidance of just one voice—hers and her professional partner and husband, Nicolae.

Over the six years with AM, I have listened to and benefitted from numerous instructors and coaches who increased my basic dance technique and helped me overcome the bigger issues of facing fears and . . . (well, if you have arrived at this page then you understand my personal challenges). I owe the foundational years of my ballroom dance journey to the AM staff and am profoundly grateful for their tutelage. Now, it was time to focus on one voice and I chose to be challenged in new ways through the professional team of Bella and Nicolae.

Dancing with Jesus:

Though I came early to the *I want to listen to one voice* point in my journey with Jesus, there were similar tugs on my heart that refined my focus on listening primarily to the voice of Jesus. There can be a tendency to listen to what religious leaders, speakers, and others (even friends) say about Jesus and their interpretations of what He said.

There are also societal voices that many listen to who have not taken the time to actually become a disciple (student) of Jesus but willingly offer their uninformed opinion as to who Jesus is. There may be some good, even accurate, information and insights about Jesus, but nothing compares to a real, authentic, consistent, and vibrant personal relationship with Jesus. Through His Spirit residing in me, I can commune with Him and be guided and transformed by His words without relying on others' viewpoints or journeys.

While he was still speaking, a bright cloud covered them, and a voice from the cloud said, 'This is My Son, whom I love; with Him I am well pleased. Listen to Him!' (Matthew 17:5). My *dance with Jesus* is personal to me and I choose to primarily listen to His voice through His Spirit and words recorded in the Bible.

From Grace to Grace:

Our role as a follower and student of Jesus is to tell people about Him, bring them to Him and to encourage them in their walk, teaching them His words. But it is liberating to know that by His *Grace* their relationship with Jesus is their own journey and that you are not responsible to fill the role of Jesus in their lives. You are not a substitute for their own search and exploration of God's word.

My two main missions in life are the following: 1) *Tell them about Me!* So, I say, *Come and see my Jesus. Could it be that He is the Messiah?* (John 4:29). 2) *Listen to Him! Listen to His voice!* (John 10:4-5, 16, 27). Why? Because *He alone is the Way, and the Truth, and the Life* (John 14:6). Only HIS voice matters to followers of, and *dancers with Jesus*.

Onwards and upwards

On the Dance Floor:

This may be the final entry for this book—or at least for some time—as I begin a new chapter in my dance journey. This page could also be titled *Keep on Dancing* as a reminder to myself that I am a dancer and will continue to dance as long as I am physically able to.

The reason I chose the phrase *Onwards and Upwards* is that *onwards* implies moving forward, one step at a time, one day at a time—through easy times and through difficult times. *Onwards!*

Upwards implies a spiritual ascent. As we keep moving forward—*onwards*—in time, we will rise in accomplishment, in victory, and eventually with a heavenly ascent. *Upwards* reminds me of the hope of the eternal future as I continue to move forward.

Dancing with Jesus:

Onwards and Upwards is also my motto when it comes to my *dance with Jesus*. Every single day, I choose to move forward toward Jesus—through the times when *all is well* and also through the *valley of the shadow of death*. Eventually, at my last breath, I know that I have the promise of *dancing with Jesus* for eternity.

If the Spirit of Him who raised Jesus from the dead dwells in you, He who raised Christ Jesus from the dead will also give life to your mortal bodies through His Spirit who dwells in you (Romans 8:11).

He who has begun a good work in you will complete it until the day of Jesus Christ (Philippians 1:6).

From Grace to Grace:

Because you have been given and experienced *Grace* through a relationship with Jesus, your role in life is to offer *gracious* encouragement to others as they journey through life. *Onwards* is a reminder to keep moving forward toward the ultimate *Upwards* hope of eternity.

Encourage others to keep moving forward with endurance, keeping their eyes on Jesus (Hebrews 12:1-2). And remind them that Jesus says He will be with us until the end (Matthew 28:20).

So, my final summary statement: *Onwards and upwards! Keep on dancing with, and for Jesus!*

FREE DANCING

A year or two has transpired since my last entry. In fact, I thought that *Onwards and Upwards* would be the final page of the book. But after sharing a rough draft with my new coach, Bella, she said, *It's not finished. In some ways, your dance journey is just beginning. You have conquered your fears and are dancing freely.*

It's true. My dance journey with new coaches Bella and Nicolae comes from an expression of dancing freely. Foundational skills and muscle memory had been established, and I danced more confidently and freely.

My window of physicality is narrowing, and as of this entry, I am now 64 years young. But I'm grateful to be challenged with bigger expressions of movement, more complex tricks, and lifts. My coaches believe in me, and I trust that when they give me a more complicated layer of movement, they will help me to be successful.

This section will feature the highlights of this phase of dancing freely. This season of my dance journey began with a focus on learning five new Rhythm dances (cha-cha, rumba, swing, bolero, and mambo) in preparation for my first competition at the independent level. Then, I added four new Smooth routines (waltz, fox trot, tango, and Viennese waltz) in anticipation of a competition that, unfortunately, was canceled due to a pandemic. For three months I was unable to dance but was determined to become even stronger when lessons resumed.

The return to the studio for lessons was joyful, even though competitions were still on hold. During this time, I began learning choreography for a Viennese waltz show routine. This is when I felt the most free to dance, especially to a specific song of my choice (*Rescue* by Lauren Daigle).

This chapter in my dance journey builds on the previous levels. My new dance Pro, Nicolae, is layering on additional techniques. The structure of each dance is similar, but now with *free dance,* I can make personal choices to do my styling and relax and breathe while dancing more freely.

Every day is a gift. And every day that I am able to dance is a gift.

Newcomer, Bronze, Silver, and Gold

On the Dance Floor:

With every aspect of learning, there is a progression from basics to mastery. A child's growth includes a continual trajectory of crawling to toddling, walking, running, and jumping.

My dance journey began as a Newcomer with the basics of ballroom dance and because of my persistence and consistency through the years, I can look back and see the progress I've made over the years. Just as a parent looks back at photos of a child, the progression of growth over time becomes more clear.s

Dancing with Jesus:

It is comforting to know that Jesus understands the physical and spiritual growth process. He, too, *grew in wisdom and stature, and in favor with God and man* (Luke 2:40, 52).

Jesus gave leaders in the Church so that believers can *become mature, attaining to the whole measure of the fullness of Christ . . . and we will grow to become in every respect the mature body of Him who is the head, that is, Christ* (Ephesians 4:11-16).

In fact, there is an *expectation* that we grow spiritually. The author of Hebrews chided some believers for *remaining 'babies' who needed to be taught again the basic things of God's word. Those who mature, who through training, have the skill to recognize the difference between right and wrong* (Hebrews 5:12-14).

Just as a child naturally grows into maturity, when we follow Jesus, our desire is to *grow in the grace and knowledge of our Lord and Savior Jesus Christ* (2 Peter 3:18).

From Grace to Grace:

When you are patiently given space and *grace* to grow, you understand the growth process and can encourage others. You can provide a gracious environment for others to grow physically and develop their unique talents and gifts.

You can also adopt a *gracious* presence of *expecting* a person's spiritual growth, especially as you begin to understand that those who *dance with Jesus* are involved in a transformational journey with Him and are growing more into His likeness.

Commencement

On the Dance Floor:

Commencement means a beginning or start, an act of starting out or blazing a new trail. It is sometimes accompanied by a graduation that celebrates a chapter or season that has been completed.

My dance commencement began after I started a new chapter under the tutelage of Bella and Nicolae. The foundation had been laid, and now I was blazing a new trail with Team Bella/Nicolae.

Dancing with Jesus:

We don't hear much about Jesus from the age of twelve until His ministry began, but there was a specific time when *He started preaching and told those listening to repent because the kingdom of heaven was near* (Matthew 4:17). After a foundational period with Jesus, *the disciples started telling everyone to turn to God* (Mark 6:12).

After Jesus died and was resurrected, the apostles were sent to share the message of the Good News, and *many men and women started having faith in the Lord* (Acts 5:14). After a dramatic conversion, Saul, also called Paul, *started telling people that Jesus is the Son of God* (Acts 9:19-21).

Our spiritual commencement begins when we turn to Jesus. *Just as Christ was buried and raised from the dead, we are buried with Jesus through baptism into death. When we come up out of the water, through the glory of the Father, we too may live a new life* (Romans 6:4).

Anyone who belongs to Christ is a new person, a new creation (2 Corinthians 5:17). Now we begin our commencement and *put on a new self, created to be like God in true righteousness and holiness* (Ephesians 4:24). At commencement, we *put on a new self which is being renewed in the image of its Creator* (Colossians 3:10).

From Grace to Grace:

We celebrate commencement at various stages of our lives. While graduation is a celebration of the finishing a season or chapter in schooling (such as graduation from high school), it is also a time to recognize that the previous chapter of learning is a launching pad to the next season of learning.

We all should be lifelong learners and encourage others to continue to develop their talents and use them to serve others.

My debut

On the Dance Floor:

Team Bella/Nicolae doted on me as their sole focus and prepared me for my first competition. Bella arranged a professional spray tan appointment, and then personally bronzed my legs. Her favorite makeup and hair stylist was scheduled just for me. Nicolae gave me an overview of the facility, and then we briefly rehearsed the routines. As ballroom dance champions, it was apparent they were familiar with this competition sphere and comfortable with all aspects of the event. They knew the organizers and spoke in Russian to the vendors whom they personally knew.

This new experience could have been intimidating for me, but I relaxed knowing that Team Bella/Nicolae's goal was to make me look and dance with confidence.

Dancing with Jesus:

God presented Jesus as the sacrifice for sin. People are made right with God when they believe that Jesus sacrificed His life, shedding His blood. He did this to show His righteousness (Romans 3:25).

Jesus loved the church (His believers) and gave Himself up to make her holy . . . and to present her to Himself as a radiant church . . . holy and blameless (Ephesians 5:25-27). *God reconciled us by Christ's body through death to present us holy in His sight* (Colossians 1:22).

God raised Jesus from the dead and will also raise us with Jesus and present His believers to Himself. This is so that the grace that is given may cause thanksgiving to overflow to the glory of God (2 Corinthians 4:14-15).

From Grace to Grace:

It is such a blessing to have a team focused on personal success. We can all play important roles in the success of another. One of my favorite roles to play is a grandmother on the team that supports the parents of my grandchildren. By joining their parents (my grown kids) with intentional support, it brings joy to watch the little ones grow and flourish.

Another profound blessing is to be on a team to encourage others on their spiritual journey with Jesus.

Let's try it!

On the Dance Floor:

It has been a couple of years working with my professional Team, Bella and Nicolae, and I trust them completely in every way. I trust the progression of how they are teaching and growing my dance skills. I trust that they have my best interests at heart when they advise when and where to compete. Though it has taken time, I also trust them when they give me new choreography that includes steps and *tricks* that seem complicated and unrealistic for my skill level. They know what I am capable of and seem to be delighted to stretch me.

But, because I trust Bella and Nicolae, when they demonstrate a new sequence that includes a movement that looks impossible for me (but effortless for Bella), my response now is, *Let's try it!* I trust that Nicolae will support me and not let me fall, even though I am off balance and relying totally on his partnering skills. I choose to courageously accept the challenge, though daunting.

Dancing with Jesus:

After *dancing with Jesus* and learning to trust His understanding of my capabilities when He sends me into unfamiliar territory, I've chosen to say,

Yes, let's try it! I trust that He knows me best and will not let me fall but will support me through His Spirit wherever He sends me.

One of the most daunting assignments Jesus sent me was that of camp director for a youth camp in Minnesota. I knew I was over my head and an unlikely candidate for the mission. But I also knew that He had prepared me for the task and would be with me every step of the way. There have been numerous times throughout my 60+ years when I have chosen to courageously step through open doors, knowing that Jesus opened them and had prepared me in advance.

Jesus had prepared Paul for an assignment in Rome and appeared to him, saying, *Take courage! As you have testified about Me in Jerusalem, so you must also testify in Rome* (Acts 23:11). Paul essentially said, *Yes, Lord, let's do it!* Then he prayed for courage, knowing that witnessing about Christ would be a death sentence for him (Philippians 1:20).

There is an account in Acts 4:13 that said *when people saw the courage of Peter and John and realized that they were unschooled, ordinary men, they took note that these men had been with Jesus*. I want to be known as having uncommon courage because I have *danced with Jesus*.

From Grace to Grace:

When you have an authentic relationship with a person, they trust you, even when you challenge them. One of my consistent messages to those in my sphere is to trust Jesus. The overflow of that trust is a courageous perspective to step through open doors, conquer challenges, and explore new adventures, relying on Him to strengthen and support each step of the way.

If you think I can do it, I trust you!

On the Dance Floor:

After years of learning and competing in Smooth and Rhythm dance styles, Bella and Nicolae suggested I begin learning Latin styles of dance. This would mean that I would start from the beginning and learn five new dance styles and routines. Cha-cha, jive, and rumba would have some transfer value from Rhythm to Latin, but the remaining two dances—paso doble and samba were brand new styles for me.

There have been numerous times during learning a challenging sequence when I stopped Nicolae and asked, *Is this that hard?* His response: *Yes, it's complex, but you will get it.* Sometimes, now, he proactively tells me *Barb, this is hard, but you can do it.* Bella will demonstrate a step or styling, and I'll say out loud *Just like that!* We giggle because we know what comes easy for Bella takes time for me to come close to what she has shown me. But they believe in me, and *if they think I can do it, I trust them.*

Dancing with Jesus:

One of the most inspiring *If you think I can do it I'll try because I trust You* moments was when Jesus invited Peter to walk on the water toward Him. We love the examples of Peter because he wants to be courageous, trusting what Jesus said, because like us, we want to trust Jesus and step out when He calls.

I imagine a smile on Jesus' face when Peter bravely said, *Lord, if it is You, tell me to come to You on the water . . . Come!*

We admire Peter because he, of all the twelve disciples, actually stepped out of the boat and walked a few steps on the water. Yes, he saw the wind and began to sink. *But he tried because he trusted Jesus.* Immediately, Jesus reached out to save him from sinking and *graciously* asked, *Why did you doubt?* (Matthew 14:22-33).

In time, Jesus would refine Peter's courageous personality by empowering him with His Spirit. And through the Holy Spirit, Jesus empowers us to be courageous in word and deed when we say, *Yes, here I am, send me! I trust You!*

From Grace to Grace:

Building courage in a child goes hand-in-hand with building trust. It has been particularly rewarding to watch our grandchildren grow in bravery while mastering new experiences. They trust when their parents say, *You're ready. Try it. Trust me.*

This summer, we watched the progression of two of our grandsons overcoming the fear of jumping into the swimming pool. Courage was built when they trusted their parent to be there when they jumped into the water and submerged. Trust was built and they were able to overcome fear and realize that they would be ok, even when jumping into the deep end. After two weeks of courage, trust, and practice, confident swimmers emerged.

I refuse to derail.

On the Dance Floor:

In the Spring of 2020, the COVID-19 pandemic changed the world as we knew it. Every aspect of life was disrupted, including the *luxury* of dancing. California was more adversely impacted by the shutdowns and mandates, and my dance studio was closed for several months. Though dancing with masks was an eventual option, I chose not to return until I could dance maskless and breathe freely.

During my time away from the studio, I wrote a *note-to-self* that became my daily motivating force. *I refuse to derail.* In fact, during this shutdown, I became even stronger and healthier by the choices I made. My daughter and I worked together to produce online exercise classes for her Pure Barre studio and we also took advantage of walks and biking along the beach, thereby increasing my physical activity.

Part of my *refusing to derail* during those chaotic months included eliminating alcohol and drinking more water, and after several months, I emerged both stronger and sleeker and ready to dance again.

This was a personal choice and one I chose to fight for. Though in a situation that was not of my making and that I had no control over, it was important to me, and I was determined to prioritize my health because I valued my dance journey.

Dancing with Jesus:

As mentioned previously, dance—and *dancing with Jesus*—is simple but not easy. We are not guaranteed an easy life just because we trust Jesus. In fact, He told His followers there would be trouble and persecution (Matthew 24:9; Mark 10:30; John 15:18-19). *But take heart! Have peace because He overcame the world!* (John 16:33).

And let us not grow weary . . . for in due season we shall reap if we do not lose heart (Galatians 6:9).

James, the brother of Jesus, gave the following advice: *Consider it pure joy, my brothers and sisters, whenever you face trials of many kinds, because you know that the testing of your faith produces perseverance. Let perseverance finish its work so that you may be mature and complete, not lacking anything* (James 1:2-4).

We have been given free will and have a choice to accept the invitation to *dance with Jesus*—or to turn away and reject His offer for eternal life. We also have free will and a choice to continue our journey with Jesus. This will have to be a personal choice, as there will be opposition, maybe even from family and friends.

Thankfully, He is *for* us, not against us, and through His Spirit, we can continue our spiritual dance with Him, refusing to derail— even when suffering trials—through His strength.

From Grace to Grace:

Life guarantees trials, setbacks and obstacles. You can choose not to derail, but to persevere through the various challenges that you face by hanging on to God's *Grace*.

And when you are in a season to be encouraging to others, one of your greatest gifts is to help others not to derail, but to remain strong and faithful, even in the face of adversity or opposition.

Therefore, brothers and sisters, in all our distress and persecution we were encouraged about you because of your faith (1 Thessalonians 3:7). *Encourage one another daily, so that we won't be hardened by the deceitfulness of sin's temptation t*o derail and mistrust Jesus (Hebrews 3:13).

May the God who gives endurance and encouragement give you the same attitude of mind toward each other that Christ Jesus had (Romans 15:5).

Redeem the time.

On the Dance Floor:

During COVID restrictions, competitions were canceled. When some competitions resumed, participants were required to wear masks. (No thanks!) Team Bella/Nicolae provided opportunities to progress by scheduling a showcase and professionally filming each solo performance. My first solo was a Viennese waltz to *Rescue* by Lauren Daigle. Several months later, I danced a tango to *Phantom of the Opera* and a jive dance to *New Shoes* by Paolo Nutini.

Dancing with Jesus:

The Book of Ecclesiastes emphasizes the role that time plays in our short lives. *No one has the power over the time of their death* (Ecclesiastes 8:8). Because we do not know what will happen tomorrow (James 4:14), it is imperative that we *redeem the short amount of time* that we do have (Ephesians 5:16).

We do not know when we will stand face-to-face and give account for our use of the time, talents and gifts allotted to us (Hebrews 4:13). So, we are encouraged that if we hear Jesus' voice today, not to harden our hearts and be deceived by sin's deceptiveness (Hebrews 3:13-15). Our motivation is not based on fear. Our awe and reverence and gratitude for Jesus *inviting us to the dance of eternal life* with Him compels us to intentionally use our time, talents and gifts to honor Him.

The disciple John states this most clearly. *And now, dear children, continue in Him, so that when He appears we may be confident and unashamed before Him at His coming* (1 John 2:28).

From Grace to Grace:

The most visible representation of the quick passage of time occurs when watching a child grow. Parents may not witness it as noticeably when they are with a child on a daily basis, but I am more aware of the passage of time from my perspective as a grandparent. First of all, how is it possible for my own son to have a 6-year-old son? Secondly, the growth in development of my infant granddaughter is stunning from month to month.

It reminds me to intentionally redeem the time of pouring into the lives of these growing children and also to appreciate the narrowing length of my allotted days. My desire is to redeem the time that God has given me to love Him, dance more closely with Jesus, and love those He has put in my sphere of influence.

Please come back to dance.

On the Dance Floor:

There are a variety of life circumstances that impact our priorities and schedules. Dance requires a commitment of time and money, and events can impact either of those, causing individuals to stop prioritizing dance.

After the pandemic mandates were eased, one of my friends bemoaned the disruption of dance and expressed the difficulty of taking that first step to recommit and return to the studio. We began our dance journey about the same time, and I knew she loved dancing and benefitted from the lessons in a variety of ways.

I know how much you love to dance, please come back. Those words of encouragement inspired her to return to the studio and continue dance lessons.

Dancing with Jesus:

Jesus told a parable about a farmer planting seeds, which was the message about the Kingdom of God. Some seeds do not mature because new believers have problems, are persecuted for believing God's word, or the evil one snatches them before they can develop roots. Some seeds do not grow because the message is crowded out by the worries of this life and the lure of wealth (Matthew 13:18-23).

But we can mutually encourage each other in our faith (Romans 1:12). One way to encourage each other in our spiritual journey is to *continue to assemble together* for worship and studying God's word, especially during times that are challenging (Hebrews 10:25). *The Scriptures give us hope and encouragement as we wait patiently for God's promises to be fulfilled* (Romans 15:4).

From Grace to Grace:

We all need to be strengthened and encouraged during our life journey. Most commonly, this occurs within a community—whether within a family, job, neighborhood, church, school group, or dance community.

When we *encourage one another daily and are of one mind, we can live in peace* (Hebrews 3:13; 2 Corinthians 13:11). You can make a difference in the lives of those around you when you *encourage the disheartened, help the weak, and be patient with everyone* (1 Thessalonians 5:14). Who do you know that might need some encouragement today?

Please try better.

On the Dance Floor:

My lovely Russian coach, Bella, recently used the phrase, *Please try better*. I stopped and giggled, promising her that I would try to do better. Thankfully, I have conquered my fear of receiving corrections mostly because I have reconciled internally that my instructors want the best for me and only ask me to *try better* because they believe in my ability. AND, instruction and correction were given with pure motives and abundant *grace* (Please). I can respond with a smile—instead of self-condemnation—for not completely pleasing someone with my imperfect performance.

Dancing with Jesus:

My dance journey mirrors my journey with God. In my younger years, I grew up with a religious emphasis on doing more good works, unsure if my behavior was *good enough* or that I might fall out of favor with God. But when I began *dancing with Jesus* and observing the *Grace*-filled and non-condemning nature of His heart toward all those He encountered, I gave myself more *grace* in my spiritual walk and in everyday living.

Yes, I continually desire to *try better* to please Jesus, but it is with an awareness that He understands my human failings and struggles. While walking on earth, Jesus demonstrated *Grace* while also challenging individuals to a higher spiritual calling. He embodied *speaking truth in love* (Ephesians 4:15), meaning, *please try better* while inspiring those around Him to grow into the potential He saw in them.

From Grace to Grace:

As you experience *Grace* from Jesus, He transforms you with a secure identity in Him. You can inspire others to grow—by *trying better*—but it is spoken with love and *grace*. As you continue in your *dance with Jesus*, you are transformed into His likeness and are able to offer His words of peace, comfort, and truth to others. You can draw them into a higher sphere of growth through communicating His Love and *Grace*.

This is the new rule now.

On the Dance Floor:

As I have advanced in my dance journey, there have been numerous times when Nicolae introduced a new concept or layer of technique that seemed to contradict what I had learned. On several occasions, I would stop Nicolae and review what I previously had been taught, and he would say, *That was then; this is the new rule now.* Sometimes, he would add, *As you progress, it will also change.*

Many of these new *rules* are nuances of dance that represent my increased level of technique and ability to handle a new concept. For instance, as a beginner, I was only focused on a basic step and how my weight was on that foot. Now, Nicolae is helping me understand where my weight is—outside foot, inside foot, ball of foot, heel, big toe? If I want to progress, these *new rules* and nuances are important for me to understand so that I can dance the most beautifully and fully possible.

Dancing with Jesus:

As I have grown and progressed in my relationship with Jesus, I have walked through various stages of *rules*. Several examples of a *new rule* are when Jesus would say, *You have heard it said . . . but I say . . .* Many of these related to the original Law given to Moses that provided a foundational *first step*. But Jesus was talking about the heart behind the *first step*. For instance, Jesus expanded the commandment against adultery to say that the *new rule* was that *if any man had looked upon a woman lustfully had already committed adultery in his heart* (Matthew 5:27-28).

Other examples of a *new rule: You have heard that it was said, 'Eye for eye, and tooth for tooth.' But I tell you, do not resist an evil person. If anyone slaps you on the right cheek, turn to them the other cheek also* (Matthew 5:38-39).

You have heard that it was said, 'Love your neighbor and hate your enemy.' But I tell you, love your enemies and pray for those who persecute you (Matthew 5:43-44).

Then Peter came to Jesus and asked, "Lord, how many times shall I forgive my brother or sister who sins against me? Up to seven times?" Jesus answered, "I tell you, not seven times, but seventy times seven (Matthew 18:21-22).

The *new rule* concept progresses from the Letter of the Law to the Spirit of the Law that reflecting a deeper understanding of the intent and heart of the Law. Apostle Paul stated in Romans 7:7, *I would not have known what sin was had it not been for the law. For I would not have known what coveting really was if the law had not said, "You shall not covet.* That was the starting point, the original rule. He later said that *the Law was our guardian, a schoolmaster, until Christ came that we might be justified by faith* (Galatians 3:24).

God intended to make a new covenant with the people of Israel and with us (through our relationship with Jesus) and *He will put His laws in their hearts and write them on their minds* (Hebrews 10:16). That's the *new rule,* the new covenant that was built upon the foundation of the original covenant.

From Grace to Grace:

As you grow and progress in your life, there are various stages when you layer higher levels of understanding on the *rules* that guide you. In theory, your maturity progresses from knowing about something to understanding the *why*, or the heart, behind the rule.

An example would be when we teach our children to share. The first level is to share because we are told by our parents. As we mature and are taught the heart underlying the *rule*, we share with others because we are learning to love others. That is the *new rule*. The intent was always behind the original rule, but it takes maturity to develop and to live from the heart and intent of love for God and love for others.

Fill up the space.

On the Dance Floor:

As I grew into more advanced levels of dance, there were aspects that were increasingly challenging. Even though my partner and I were dancing in closer body contact, Nicolae also explained that as I created more space with my body position, he was able to move more fully within that space. My upper body is positioned away from my partner to allow for fuller, larger movements. Arm movements are extended and widened for a fuller presentation as I fill up the space.

The result of creating more space and filling the space is that the movement is more dynamic, energetic, and compelling to watch.

Dancing with Jesus:

Spiritually, we can choose to create space in our lives for Jesus to move. Just as in dance, we stay connected to Jesus but are more open to His lead and prepared to react to His lead when He initiates a direction.

As I have opened my awareness of Jesus' lead and surrendered to where He wants to lead me, there is a fullness in life that reflects His desire that we *live life* [that only He gives] *to the full* (John 10:10).

As we create space for Him to move within, *from His fullness we have received Grace upon Grace* (John 1:16).

I pray that out of his glorious riches He may strengthen you with power through His Spirit in your inner being, so that Christ may dwell in your hearts through faith. And I pray that you, being rooted and established in love, may have power, together with all the Lord's holy people, to grasp how wide and long and high and deep is the love of Christ, and to know this love that surpasses knowledge—that you may be filled to the measure of all the fullness of God (Ephesians 3:16-19).

From Grace to Grace:

Most of us live *small*, not realizing what *living life to the full* looks like. You can choose to trust that He has your best interests at heart and is able to direct your movements. You will grow in confidence and move more fully as you receive *Grace* upon *Grace.*

As you become acquainted with the heart of Jesus—that He desires for each individual to live fully in their created potential—you can encourage others to create space for Jesus to move.

Hold your core.

On the Dance Floor:

Visiting professional Michael Mead made an impact on me by emphasizing the theme of *holding your core*. He said that as I relied on Nicolae and used his stability like that of a ballet barre, I would be able to have fuller movements. My Leader provides stability as I stay connected and *hold my core*.

Movement comes from the torso, the body's core. Arms and feet movement follow after the body's core is strong.

Michael Mead encouraged me by saying, *You have more potential than you know or understand.* I wanted to cry because of his words. He also challenged me with the shocking statement, *If you do not keep moving toward your potential as a dancer, you are depriving the audience of a beautiful performance.* He likened watching our ballroom dancing partnership to an inspiring Olympic performance.

Dancing with Jesus:

The core of our existence is Jesus. *In Him we live and move and have our being* (Acts 17:28). Our core—our heart or being—is for Jesus first. The movement of our feet, arms, and hands—our serving, doing—follows from the connection to the heart of Jesus.

Because our core is in Jesus, it is important to remember that it is *God who makes us stand firm in Christ* (2 Corinthians 1:21). There are several scriptures that remind us to *stand firmly in our identity with Jesus* (Philippians 4:1) and to *stand firmly and fully assured and in everything God wills* (Colossians 4:12). *Stand firm in the faith* (1 Peter 5:9) and *be patient and stand firm, because the Lord's coming is near* (James 5:8).

From Grace to Grace:

If you have read through my journey to this point, you may have noticed that though there are many applications that apply to our human relationships, my main focus as it relates to my human relationships is to encourage others to *stand tall and firm in their core identity and foundation in Jesus*. This is helpful in our daily reality, but eventually, those who have accepted Jesus' *invitation to dance* with Him will enter into the reality of eternity in His presence.

Different expressions of music

On the Dance Floor:

My dance journey is fueled by the desire to be able to express in body movement what stirs in my heart when I hear any style of music. To dance freely means to understand the mood or message of the music and be able to move in a way that expresses the music. Because there is a variety of music, there are numerous dance styles that capture the mood of the music. Examples include the fun swing, intense tango, heartbreaking or endearing waltz, and upbeat, playful foxtrot.

When talking to Bella about the passion inherent in her Russian culture, I shared that music by composers Rachmaninoff and Tchaikovsky elicits an ache to physically express what their music inspires deep within my heart. Argentine Tango is another style of music and dance that moves my soul, and I was able to explore this style during a solo performance with Nicolae at an annual studio dinner party.

Dancing with Jesus:

Though we are given *different gifts, according to the grace given to each of us* (Romans 12:6), many times we will be called into an area that is not naturally as comfortable. This gives us an opportunity to grow into a more complete representation of the multifaceted Jesus.

I have come to be open to walking through a variety of new and open doors (gifts) that Jesus presents to me, knowing that if He called me into a new growth opportunity, *He will equip me to use that new gift to serve others* (1 Peter 4:10).

We are encouraged to *grow in grace and knowledge of our Lord and Savior Jesus Christ* (2 Peter 3:18) and to continue *growing into maturity, into the stature of the fullness of Christ* (Ephesians 4:13).

From Grace to Grace:

Though you may have a natural proclivity and talent and/or have been given a specific gift, you can continually grow in other areas. You can encourage those in your sphere to also explore new experiences and step through open doors that stretch, grow, and mature them.

1 + 1 = 1 (in dance)

On the Dance Floor:

Numerous times Nicolae would say something that was similar to a statement I heard as a Newcomer, but with a higher-level nuance. A couple of the first Sergisms that I made note of were: *You can dance more fully with two than with one* and *The goal of the dance couple is to move as a unit.*

When Nicolae said that *1 + 1 = 1 in dance*, it took some time to understand the nuance. In all the three statements, there are two individuals, but in this new equation of *1 + 1 = 1* the number 2 does not appear or is implied. There is only *oneness*.

As a dance partnership develops, the seamless connection between partners creates the appearance of only 1 person dancing. There is no distinction or separation into individuals, just consistent and continual movement of 1. Two individuals are now dancing in complete unity and we are privileged to witness *1 + 1 = 1 in dance.*

Dancing with Jesus:

Nicolae's statement of *1 + 1 = 1 in dance* helped me understand when Jesus said, *the Father and I are One* (John 10:30).

$1 + 1 = 1$ (in God's sphere) captures the uniqueness of each 1 in the partnership. And as in the goal of dance, with God there is complete unity, seamless connection and *oneness* that we don't witness 2 separate entities, but 1 unit—*one*.

If we carry that further, in God's sphere $1 + 1 + 1 = 1$. The Father, Jesus and Holy Spirit are one. There is complete unity, seamless connection and oneness. We might witness or experience aspects of the unique entities but are reminded of the 1 unit—*one*. We may say *three in one* . . . yes . . . nuanced, but $1 + 1 + 1 = 1$.

Hear, O Israel: The LORD our God, the LORD is one (Deuteronomy 6:4). Other translations: *The LORD our God is one LORD;* or *The LORD is our God, the LORD is one;* or *The LORD is our God, the LORD alone.* Nuanced. Honestly, it will take me a lifetime and eternity to truly understand God's equation of *oneness*.

From Grace to Grace:

A similar, but nuanced application of $1 + 1 = 1$ is the marriage relationship that was created in the beginning (Genesis 2:24). *That is why a man leaves his father and mother and is united to his wife, and they become one flesh.* Jesus affirmed the intent of marriage by quoting Genesis 2:24 and adding another layer. *For this reason a man will leave his father and mother and be united to his wife, and the two will become one flesh. So, they are no longer two, but one flesh* (Mark 10:7-9). $1 + 1 = 2 = 1$.

Oneness in any relationship is complicated and challenging, but God has given us a goal of *oneness* of our relationships and gave us the example of Jesus and the Father.

Pass by me; surpass me

On the Dance Floor:

There have been several step sequences when Nicolae told me to move/step directly toward or into him. He would say, *Don't worry about running into me; I'll step aside. Pass by me. Surpass me. I'll catch up.*

Not only does this moving forward toward my Leader require me to trust that he will step aside and let me pass by him, but I accept that it is ok to be ahead of him. Though we are dancing as a unit, there are occasions when we trade positions, and I, as the Follower, am now in the front or lead position. When this occurs, the size of my steps and the direction of my turns determine the position on the floor, and my partner adjusts so that we continue to dance in unison.

Dancing with Jesus:

As a follower of Jesus, I'm baffled and challenged by His statement, *Whoever believes in me will do the works I have been doing, and they will do even greater things than these, because I am going to the Father* (John 14:12).

Some explain His statement by implying that collectively, as His followers, we will do greater works. Jesus did works and miracles as one person and now there are collectively millions with His Spirit, and this is what it means to do greater works. Yes . . . AND . . .

As a dancer with Jesus, the statement made by my human dance partner Nicolae gave me a new perspective. Maybe Jesus implied, *Come to Me. Step toward Me. Keep moving forward toward Me. I'm sending you. Go! I'll step aside. Pass by Me. I'm right here and will never leave you on your own. Surpass Me. Do greater works!*

Really? You mean for me to heal others in Your name, cast out demons and restore broken people through the power of Your Holy Spirit?

Peter and the apostles were empowered by the Holy Spirit and *performed many signs and wonders among the people . . . more and more men and women believed in the Lord and were added to their number. As a result, people brought the sick into the streets and laid them on beds and mats so that at least Peter's shadow might fall on some of them as he passed by. Crowds gathered also from the towns around Jerusalem, bringing their sick and those tormented by impure spirits, and all of them were healed* (Acts 5:12-16).

God did extraordinary miracles through Paul, so that even handkerchiefs and aprons that had touched him were taken to the sick, and their illnesses were cured, and the evil spirits left them (Acts 19:11-12).

Would those two examples of Peter and Paul be considered *greater works?* I'm not sure. And I'm certainly not sure what it all means to me personally, but I do know Jesus is calling me—and all His believers—to go and do more than what we limit ourselves to.

From Grace to Grace:

As parents and/or mentors, we pour ourselves into those around us and are expectantly waiting to see how they pass by us and surpass us, building on what we provided as a foundation. And we smile while watching them shine.

In a similar sense, I believe Jesus smiles when He sends us out and watches us reflect Him and do the works (maybe even *greater works?*) that He did.

You're ready!

On the Dance Floor:

Nicolae and I began preparing for our annual dance studio dinner event six weeks prior to the date. Each dance student would perform a solo routine of the dance style and music of her or his choice. I decided to perform a bolero routine to a Russian song that particularly intrigued me. Because I had been concentrating on Smooth dance routines for competition the past year, preparation for the solo required reconstructing a bolero routine and revisiting bolero technique. It almost seemed like I was starting from scratch because it had been so long since I danced the bolero.

As the date quickly approached, I questioned whether I would be ready to perform and tried to overcome my anxiety. Nicolae initially assured me, *You'll be ready.* It seemed he had more confidence in me than I did. A couple weeks before the big day, he began to tell me, *You're ready.* I didn't feel ready. I knew that my routine might not be perfect—and I only had one chance to dance my best in front of an audience composed of dance aficionados. But I trusted my coach and changed my internal conversation. I began to tell myself, *You're ready!*

Dancing with Jesus:

I would imagine that Jesus' disciples and followers did not feel ready when He sent them out with instructions on what they were to do and with the authority to heal the sick and cast out demons (Mark 6:1-12; Luke 10:1-24). Would they have responded, *You want us to do what?!!* Jesus would not have appointed them and sent them out unless He knew they were ready.

Did they have complete success or do everything perfectly? No. In fact, one father came to Jesus, saying that His disciples were unable to heal his son of severe seizures (Matthew 17:14-21). Jesus didn't chide His disciples for their inability but used their *failure* as an opportunity for further instruction.

After Jesus was resurrected, He gave them His final instructions and a profound reminder. *All authority in heaven and on earth has been given to me. Therefore, go and make disciples of all nations, baptizing them in the name of the Father and of the Son and of the Holy Spirit, and teaching them to obey everything I have commanded you. And surely I am with you always, to the very end of the age* (Matthew 28:18-20).

Thankfully, when Jesus sends me out on His behalf, He does with *Grace. Barb, you're ready. Go!* I trust Him and believe that He trusts me, even in my incompleteness. And I'm assured that no matter where He sends me, He says that *He will never leave me or forsake me* (Hebrews 13:5).

From Grace to Grace:

One of the most encouraging and empowering expressions we can speak to others is, *You're ready!* A child may feel afraid to walk, to go to school, to try something new or meet new friends. By reassuring them that they have what it takes and that they are ready, we encourage and inspire growth.

And when a child, family member or friend tries something new and they fall or don't do it correctly or completely, we *graciously* continue to encourage them to try again, inspiring them to grow.

Everything ugly can become beautiful.

On the Dance Floor:

Professional dancers make every movement look natural and uncontrived. If a photograph were taken at any moment of a sequence or routine, the symmetrical artistry would be captured.

But for me, it seems that my arm and hand styling feel the least natural and takes the longest to intentionally craft into dance movement. There was one sequence in a tango routine where I couldn't figure out what to do with my hands. I mentioned to Nicolae that I felt awkward and gawky and wanted to fix it. He told me not to worry about it because *everything ugly can become beautiful,* and the section I felt uncomfortable with actually resolved into a beautiful finishing pose.

That definitely was a reassuring statement, but I'm still trying to figure out what to do with my arms and hands to look effortlessly beautiful.

Dancing with Jesus:

It cannot be said that Jesus was *ugly*. In my opinion, His heart and Love for His creation was stunningly *beautiful*.

But . . . The Cross . . . Roman crucifixion was designed to be the most traumatic and humiliating punishment devised. Jesus was hammered to a cross after He had been brutally beaten and scourged beyond recognition.

And only because Jesus was willing to submit to the cross do we have life—if we accept His *ugly* to become *beautiful.* Our *ugliness* because of our sin has been redeemed into the *beauty* of His righteousness.

God made him who had no sin to be sin for us, so that in Him we might become the righteousness of God (2 Corinthians 5:21). *He himself bore our sins in His body on the cross, so that we might die to sins and live for righteousness; by His wounds you have been healed* (1 Peter 2:24).

The message of the cross is foolishness for some and a stumbling block for others (1 Corinthians 1:18-25). But when we understand the implications of Jesus submitting Himself to *the offense of the Cross,* we gratefully accept the beauty of His sacrifice (Galatians 5:11).

Jesus reconciled to Himself all things by making peace through His blood shed on the cross (Colossians 1:20). We trust Him to create *beauty instead of ashes and praise dancing and joy instead of mourning and despair* (Isaiah 61:3).

From Grace to Grace:

There are times in our lives and in the lives of our family and friends that look like ashes because of our own failings or the ugliness of others. There are times of mourning and despair. But Jesus can turn those ashes into a work of beauty. And once again there can be joy and dancing where there was grief.

When others are going through difficult seasons you can encourage them with hopeful words. In time—and only made possible by the beauty of Jesus—all things will be redeemed and be made new.

Then I saw a new heaven and a new earth, for the first heaven and the first earth had passed away, and there was no longer any sea. I saw the Holy City, the new Jerusalem, coming down out of heaven from God, prepared as a bride beautifully dressed for her husband. And I heard a loud voice from the throne saying, Look! God's dwelling place is now among the people, and he will dwell with them. They will be his people, and God himself will be with them and be their God. 'He will wipe every tear from their eyes. There will be no more death' or mourning or crying or pain, for the old order of things has passed away (Revelation 21:1-4).

Competition mode

On the Dance Floor:

A couple weeks prior to a competition, the dynamic in the studio changes. Nicolae seriously kicks in into a higher level of intensity and the chit-chat, banter and level of fun changes when we are in competition mode. We understand that his intensity in the studio increases because he wants us to perform at our highest potential and he uses this strategy to prepare us for the real dance floor.

We begin to rehearse rounds of *finals*, as if replicating the actual competition. This means that routines are performed back-to-back in sequence to build up endurance. A Smooth round includes waltz, tango, foxtrot and Viennese waltz; Rhythm includes cha-cha, rumba, swing, bolero and mambo; Latin routines are cha-cha, rumba, jive, paso doble and samba.

Not only is muscle memory required, but each round is a non-stop series of the particular style. Each routine can range from 1 to 1 ½ minutes in length so a typical final round ranges from 5 to 6 minutes with no breaks or repeats for mistakes. The goal of rehearsing a round of finals is to replicate the energy and performance level as if on the dance floor while being judged.

Nicolae prepares us the best he can in the practice studio, knowing that the intensity of actual competition is increased when lights, gowns, judges, spectators and numerous competitors sharing a dance floor are added to the equation.

Dancing with Jesus:

As we read John chapters 12-17, the tone of Jesus changed. Though He said His soul was troubled, what He was facing—the Cross—was the reason He came to earth.

The weeks and days leading up to Jesus' trial intensified for the disciples because of the seriousness of Jesus. They were not fully aware of what their beloved leader was going to face, but He gave them final words of instruction and warning before He was going away. He warned them about betraying Him when in the midst of His trial. As much as He prepared them when the reality of the trial and His death became personal, they floundered.

Thankfully, in His loving *Grace* they were reassured and restored after He conquered the grave and appeared to them. He gave them instructions to wait for the Holy Spirit (Acts 1:1-5). It was almost time for them to be sent out into the world among proverbial wolves (Matthew 10:16) and He prepared them the best He could. But only when the reality of being sent out on their own without Him—but with His Spirit—would they experience the outcome of their preparation.

From Grace to Grace:

There are numerous times when a parent and/or mentor determines that preparation and instruction are finished. The foundation has been laid and it's almost time for their child or student to be launched. Final instructions are given before going to school, learning to drive, traveling solo, going to college or counseling for marriage.

As the time for the launch draws closer, instruction becomes more serious because there is a lot at stake. Though those under your care and tutelage may not understand or appreciate your intensity of preparation, you take it seriously because you desire success for those you love.

Muscle memory

On the Dance Floor:

Hours and weeks are poured into preparing for a competition. The closer we get to the actual event; it is important that muscle memory is established and kicks in. But there are times when Nicolae will remind me, *You're thinking too much! Don't think—feel. Trust your muscle memory!*

When on the competition floor, the two things I can trust are my partner and my muscle memory. It is time to let go of thinking mode. Instead, it is time to feel the music and enjoy the moment.

Dancing with Jesus:

Jesus gave His disciples final instructions before His departure on earth. They had spent years, months, days and hours walking with Jesus, hearing Scripture and His words. The foundation had been laid. *Whenever you are arrested and brought to trial, do not worry beforehand about what to say.*

Just say whatever is given you at the time, for it is not you speaking, but the Holy Spirit (Mark 13:11).

Their *muscle memory* would come from the Holy Spirit Who would empower them in a few short weeks. Jesus reminded them to *remain in Him because He was in them. Without Him they could do nothing* (John 15:1-5). Jesus told them they would *testify about Him because they had been with Him from the beginning* (John 15:27). But they wouldn't be left alone. The *Holy Spirit would guide them into all the truth* (John 16:12-15).

Holy Spirit will also guide *us* into truth. We lay a strong foundation by reading Scripture and focusing on the words of Jesus. When we find ourselves in a situation where we don't know what to do, we can rely on the Holy Spirit to bring to remembrance His words and to give us the words that we might be unable to conjure ourselves.

Because the mouth speaks out of the abundance and overflow of the heart (Matthew 12:34), we ask Jesus for transformation of our *heart memory* that reflects Him.

From Grace to Grace:

It is important to lay truthful and deep foundations in every aspect of our lives so that when situations arise that require us to *not think, but react,* we can rely on muscle *memory* to help us make the right decisions and actions. Remember that you also have access to the Holy Spirit, through the gift from Jesus, to help you. As your heart is transformed to more truly reflect the heart of Jesus, your *heart memory* will overflow with His words of truth and peace.

He's our main man.

On the Dance Floor:

If I feel that preparing for competition is personally challenging, I remind myself that Nicolae is dancing with multiple women throughout the several days of competition. He is preparing physically for the demanding schedule of dancing hundreds of rounds, and as our professional partner, he remembers every routine for each of his students. It truly is remarkable!

The students are sweating. So is Nicolae. Occasionally, he gets grazed by a misguided arm or stepped on. Yes, we contestants play an important role in our competition, but the majority of the weight is on Nicolae's shoulders. We want to please him and try our best but know that he wants our success even more than we do.

Dancing with Jesus:

When Jesus lived on earth, He experienced the reality of everyday living—hunger, exhaustion, sweat and tears. *He was fully human in every way . . . because He suffered, He is able to help those who suffer* (Hebrews 2:14-18). He personally saw and knew every person who crossed His path and willingly and *graciously* took time to heal, to restore, to cast out evil spirits, to rescue, and to provide for. He restored physically, socially, relationally, and most importantly, He restored each of us spiritually by paying the price for our sin and reconciling us to the Father.

In Jesus we have redemption through His blood, the forgiveness of sins, in accordance with the riches of God's grace that He lavished on us (Ephesians 1:3-8).

We see Jesus, who was made lower than the angels for a little while, now crowned with glory and honor because He suffered death, so that by the grace of God He might taste death for everyone. In bringing many sons and daughters to glory, it was fitting that God, for whom and through whom everything exists, should make the pioneer of their salvation perfect through what He suffered (Hebrews 2:9-10).

Jesus is, and has been, and always will be our Main Man! He bore the weight of sin on the cross for each individual and for the world so that those who accept His Love and *Grace* would enjoy eternal life dancing with Him.

From Grace to Grace:

Therefore,

Now may the God of peace, who through the blood of the eternal covenant brought back from the dead our Lord Jesus, that great Shepherd of the sheep, equip you with everything good for doing His will, and may He work in us what is pleasing to Him, through Jesus Christ, to whom be glory for ever and ever. Amen (Hebrews 13:20-21).

I'm a ballroom dancer.

On the Dance Floor:

Over ten years ago I stepped into a dance studio and began my adventure with ballroom dance. No one invited me into the journey, I just felt the tug and knew in my heart it was something I wanted to do. Maybe I also sensed I *needed* to explore dance because there was something missing in my life.

Little did I know then how much ballroom dance would become part of my identity—who I became, who I am. But it took me several years before I would confidently say *I'm a ballroom dancer* when describing not only *what I do* but *who I am*. Ballroom dance is so integral to my personal growth and identity that I cannot separate the joy I receive from dancing from the role it has played in my life.

Dancing with Jesus:

Numerous times Jesus said to those He encountered, *Follow Me*. There was an invitation to be identified with Him—spiritually to *believe in Him and have eternal life in Him* (John 3:15-16) and to literally follow Him and do what He said (John 14:15, 21). Our identity eternally will be connected to Jesus if we are a believer and followers of Jesus.

In Him we love and move and have our being (Acts 17:28). If we believe in Jesus and in what He provided for us—forgiveness, reconciliation, eternal life—our entire identity will be in Him forever.

It has taken me some time to fully understand and correctly communicate my identity which includes *what I do*, but more importantly *who I am. I am a follower of Jesus.*

Some might ask, A*re you a Christian?* Yes, but more accurately stated, *I am a follower of Jesus. In Him I love and move and have my being. Because I live in Him, I live for Him. Out of my being in Jesus comes my doing for Jesus.*

From Grace to Grace:

There is an overwhelming proclivity when getting acquainted with a person to ask, *What do you do?* Maybe we should be asking the more important questions: *Who are you? What is the essence of your being?* When you know the centrality of a person's identity of *being*, then you will better understand the overflow of their *being* into their *doing*.

Of greater importance is helping individuals discover or rediscover their identity in Jesus—the Eternal Son of God who provides true identity through believing in Him and following Him eternally. When you say, *I'm a follower of Jesus*, you identify with His Love and *Grace* which overflows into every aspect of *who you are* and *what you do*.

My collection of dresses

On the Dance Floor:

During the ten years of my dance journey, I have collected a variety of dresses and costumes that represent a specific chapter or event that was uniquely special and memorable. I knew my first Smooth dress would have to be *sapphire blue* because that was the color of the dress I wore in the dream when Jesus asked me to dance with Him (and my birthstone is sapphire, and I love blue). Because embellished ballroom dresses are very expensive, I wore my beautiful blue dress for several years until I knew it was time for a new dress to represent a higher level of dance. Bold *red* was the color I chose for my next Smooth dress because it made me dance more bravely (and because I had become more courageous).

When I began to dance Rhythm, I selected a *yellow and black* dress that I could also wear for All-round (Smooth and Rhythm) competitions. Then I upgraded my Rhythm dress to a *green* dress with feathers. That was a fun and playful season.

When I began a new chapter with Team Bella/Nicolae, Bella helped me design a Rhythm dress with a designer in Russia, and it was the dress I wore at my debut competition with Team Bella/Nicolae. When competitions reopened after the pandemic, I decided to dance Smooth style again and wanted a new dress to represent another chapter, so Bella helped me design a *white and purple dress*.

Bella loaned me one of her Latin dresses to dance at my first competition in Latin. In my last Smooth competition, Bella and I designed a dress inspired by Princess Cinderella and selected the color *turquoise*.

Along the way I have also collected a variety of dresses and costumes for specific featured dances or events. In my closet, you will find a 50s outfit, a country western fringe dress with cowboy boots, red dresses for tango and Argentine tango, and even a neon-colored disco pant set.

Dancing with Jesus:

When looking back on my journey with Jesus, I recall distinct and different chapters that represent growth in my relationship with Him by maturing into a more complete version of who He created me to be. Some of my most memorable and impactful chapters include a season of being Camp Director at a Christian youth camp, writing *Portrait of a Woman and Jesus*, leading women's ministry and multiple Bible studies that I wrote, and volunteering at Horizon Pregnancy Clinic.

There are also other chapters in my life that have shaped who I have become, including being married for 46 years, being a mother of three, and being a grandmother of four. Those are constant, though changing, seasons that I've walked through with Jesus.

There are chapters of brief adventures that Jesus has used to grow my courage and expose me to a variety of experiences, including sailing, playing the harp, floral arranging, and praise dance. Jesus has *graciously* provided numerous opportunities, chapters, and seasons to enrich my life in Him.

My frame was not hidden from You when I was made in the secret place, when I was woven together in the depths of the earth. Your eyes saw my unformed body; all the days ordained for me were written in Your book before one of them came to be (Psalm 139:15-16).

From Grace to Grace:

Each of us has a unique journey through life marked by numerous seasons and chapters. You can facilitate the growth in another by encouraging her or him to take advantage of opportunities that, though challenging, are designed to add layers to the potential that God created them to become. It is an honor to witness the journey of *becoming* and celebrate the unique trajectory of each of our family and friends.

She's one of mine.

Dancing with Jesus:

Recently, I had a prayer vision where Jesus was leading me down an elevated walkway into the presence of my heavenly Father. An audience was standing on both sides of the walkway observing the procession. Jesus quietly said to me, *I want to show you off. You're beautiful.* I knew it wasn't my physical beauty Jesus was commenting on, though I was glowing with confidence from being with Him. As we approached the throne, Jesus said to His Father, *She is one of Mine.*

Though this was a personal encounter for me, I also felt internal joy, knowing that others, including my sisters-in-Christ, were also His.

As I approached the Father there was an overwhelming sense of confidence in my posture. *I'm one of His!* Of myself, I was not capable or qualified to stand in the presence of the Father. But it was only because Jesus chose me and paid the penalty of sin for me that I would be reconciled and presentable to the Holy Father.

[Insert: I've been devoted to God since my youth, but it was only during a profound spiritual awakening that I experienced the *Grace* of Jesus. As I shared at the beginning of this book, my intimate journey began when Jesus asked me to *dance with Him*. But during the ten years since stepping into the dance studio, I have been deeply transformed by the Love and *Grace* of Jesus. While *dancing with Him*, there has been no hint of fear, timidity, self-doubt, self-condemnation, shame, or guilt. Only Love was projected through Him into my heart.]

So, when Jesus spoke the words, *She's one of Mine* in my prayer vision, I experienced an interesting and complementing wave of feelings—humility, yet confidence. Instead of reflexively getting *smaller,* I stood taller, receiving His compliment as true and empowering. Though it was not clearly seen, I sensed a smile on the Father's face. He was pleased because His Son was pleased. This is *Grace*. And because I've experienced it, I can dance confidently through life, knowing that *I am one of His*.

The one who has My commands and keeps them is the one who loves Me. The one who loves Me will be loved by My Father. I will also love him and will reveal Myself to him (John 14:21).

On the Dance Floor:

Shortly after the prayer vision described above, I had the opportunity to perform a solo at our dance studio's annual event. After the performance, I received the following text messages from my dance instructors:

Nicolae: *Thank you for believing in us. You dance very good. You are our star.*

Bella: *You are superstar dancer and amazing human being. We love you and care about you.*

It is only through my instructors' willingness to invest in my dance journey that they can see progress. And it is through their patience and encouragement that I have thrived under their coaching. Of myself, I am incapable of reaching the level of dance that Bella and Nicolae have grown me into. I'm humbled and grateful. And because of their belief in me, I stand and dance more confidently in their presence.

From Grace to Grace:

The ultimate goal of our spiritual journey is to *be conformed to the image of God's Son* (Romans 8:29). The transformation into the reflection of Jesus is a lifelong journey, enhanced by the intentionality of *dancing with Jesus*, staying connected to Him, following Him, imitating Him, seeking Him, proclaiming Him and expectantly waiting for Him to return and for eternity to begin. There is no higher pursuit, no higher calling and no higher reward.

The *Grace* of *dancing in His presence* transforms a person in such a powerful way that she or he reflects the *Grace* of Jesus in everyday life. Those who are blessed to come in the sphere of *one of His* cannot help but be the recipient of *grace* because of His overflowing *Grace*.

To my fellow dancers with Jesus

But you, dear friends, by building yourselves up in your most holy faith and praying in the Holy Spirit, keep yourselves in God's love as you wait for the mercy of our Lord Jesus Christ to bring you to eternal life.

To Him who is able to keep you from stumbling and to present you before His glorious presence without fault and with great joy—to the only God our Savior be glory, majesty, power and authority, through Jesus Christ our Lord, before all ages, now and forevermore! Amen. (Jude 1:20-21, 24-25)

www.ingramcontent.com/pod-product-compliance
Lightning Source LLC
Chambersburg PA
CBHW060504090426
42735CB00011B/2100